Jennifer d'Abo

At Home

recipes for stylish people in a hurry

Jennifer d'Abo

Photographs by Michael Freeman

Drawings by Fiona Hawthorne

Home

recipes for stylish people in a hurry

Thames and Hudson

British Library Cataloguing-in-Publishing Data
A catalogue record for this book is available from the British Library

ISBN 0-500-28120-3

Printed in Hong Kong

CONTENTS

BY WAY OF INTRODUCTION

THIS BOOK WAS BORN OF TWO THINGS: my passion for food and the encouragement of those well-known publishers, Ian and Marjorie Chapman, and Stanley Baron, who finally ended up with me as his client.

I have had no formal training as a cook, or for that matter for anything else, but being able to entertain people and amuse myself in doing so has given me great pleasure. I have picked up tips and advice from talented cooks, both professional and amateur, and I have depended to a large extent on my instincts. There are many wonderful recipes here that I have collected from friends round the world and ideas from many restaurants. I hope there may be something for everyone. There are not a great many recipes for desserts or sweets as I am not a lover of them. By the same token, I am not strong on red meat recipes, since I eat little red meat myself. However, I trust there will be enough to stimulate your taste buds.

A love of good food is an expression of love of a good life. Bringing people and food together at the table is gratifying and should be done in style, combining the charms of colours, tastes, shapes, textures and smells. I only hope that I will be able to whet your appetites between these pages. I have allowed my imagination to run riot and it has been great fun. My goal is to stimulate *your* imagination.

Being a businesswoman and usually rather short of time, I believe in using all the help I can get. If there is some ready-made soup that I can tweak to make special, or cooked chicken breasts, washed and chopped vegetables, or even tomato sauce, I will use them. I can see no reason to be proud when you can use good base food to which you add your own flavours.

My thanks go to IBM for inventing 'Lily the Laptop', my friendly computer which has made all this possible. I was much too embarrassed to dictate into a machine, and my handwriting is famous for being unreadable.

My final intent is that this book should be inspirational and fun.

A FOOTNOTE TO MY AMERICAN FRIENDS

They tell me that a British cookbook needs to be 'translated' before it can be acceptable in the US market, but I wonder… I have been reading and using American cookbooks for many years and have never run into any trouble. I know that some measurements are slightly different, that the Imperial pint and quart are larger than their American counterparts, and that there are differences in some of the names and expressions we use. But, honestly, don't most serious cookbook addicts know the differences between American and British usage? With a nod to that wonderful song of the Gershwin brothers, don't they know that

you say *romaine* and we say *cos*
you say *eggplant* and we say *aubergine*
you say *beets* and we say *beetroots*
you say *filet* and we say *fillet*
you say *zucchini* and we say *courgette*
(and why can't we invent a common transatlantic English name for this delicious vegetable?)
you say *cans* and we say *tins*
you say *refrigerator* and we say *fridge*
you say *cookie* and we say *biscuit*
you say *dessert* and we say *pudding* or *sweet*
you say *chips* and we say *crisps*
we say *chips* and you say *French fries*

And you don't, sad to say, seem to grow one of my favourite vegetables, broad beans, though you can substitute limas.

I have tried to keep these anomalies down to a minimum, and I would hope you will manage to cook between the lines. As for those measurements, they are not so far out as people seem to think. For example, the Imperial pint is 20 fl. oz. and the American pint is 19. Expressed another way, the U.S. pint is ⅚ of the British pint, and the U.S. quart likewise ⅚ of the British quart. Cooking temperatures, however, can be important; and so I am setting out here a table of equivalents:

Solid Fuel	Gas (GB)	C	F	To cook
Very cool	½	110	225	stew
	½	120	250	
Cool	1	140	275	casseroles, stew, milk and egg dishes
	2	150	300	
Slow	3	160	325	biscuits
Moderate	4	180	350	bread and butter pudding
Mod. hot	5	190	375	baked tomatoes
	6	200	400	soufflés
Hot	7	220	425	fast roasts, bread
	8	230	450	puff and flaky pastry
Very hot	9	240	475	

MY STORE CUPBOARD

The following products are (hopefully) in my store cupboard all the time. I have found over the years that it is much better to store too little than too much. As most supermarkets are now open seven days a week, it is not necessary, unless you live in a very remote area, to keep a lot of stock.

I am not going to list the obvious - such as sugar, flour, dried milk, etc. - as this book is really about entertaining.

THE MUSTS

Oils and vinegars

Safflower (or sunflower) oil for
ordinary cooking

Good olive oil

Sesame oil

Basil oil

White wine vinegar

Tarragon vinegar

Vinaigre aux herbes de provence

Mustards

English, mixed and dry

Maille à l'ancienne

Grey Poupon Dijon mustard

Moutarde verte a l'estragon

Sauces

Worcestershire sauce

Chilli sauce

Thai chilli dipping sauce

Light soy sauce

Sharwoods plum sauce

Herbs and spices

Coriander

Lemon grass

Parsley

Garlic

Thyme

Rosemary

Chilli

Turmeric

Saffron

Black peppercorns

Mixed coloured peppercorns

Cloves

Basil

Barbecue seasoning

Curry pastes

Cinnamon

Nutmeg

Bits and pieces

Caperberries

Capers

Arborio rice

Packets of dried porcini mushrooms

Rahms croustades

Various pastas

Pesto sauce

Sundried tomato paste

Anchovies

Hellmann's mayonnaise

Gravy browning

Cannelloni beans

Flageolet beans

Gelatine

Japanese pink pickled ginger

Ginger root

Grated parmesan cheese

Jars of beetroot

Stock cubes

TABLE LAYING

The art of laying tables is very hard to learn. What I offer here is accepted as formal and can be quite easy to do if you understand that the principle is to start from the outside and work inwards. In other words, if you have a starter you put the spoon (if it is soup) or small knife and fork on the outside. The butter knife is put on the side plate only if it is small; if it is doubling for a cheese knife then it goes closest to the mat on the right-hand side of the place setting.

Basic table laying for a three course dinner:

Table mat

Starting from nearest to the mat and working outwards, you put a sweet/dessert spoon on the right and a fork on the left, then (for the main course) a large knife on the right and a large fork on the left. A small knife and fork or spoon (for the starter or soup) should be on the outside.
The knives and forks should all be level at the bottom and should be a 'thumb's joint' from the edge of the table.

Glasses

If you are going to have a white wine glass, red wine glass, water glass and liqueur glass, they should be placed as follows: The white wine glass should be about 2 ins. away from the top of the knives on the right side of the place setting. Behind it should be the red wine glass. The water glass should be just to the right of the red wine glass and the liqueur glass should be at the back. The reason for this is that the first three should be at a comfortable distance for your hand without stretching, and as one usually moves the liqueur glass forward after having finished the wines, it should be at the back.

Soufflés

At the beginning of a meal these should be eaten with a large fork but laid with a large knife and fork. Sweet soufflés should be laid with a spoon and a fork.

Fish

This is a difficult one! In grand houses, fish is eaten with two large forks, both laid on the left. It is said that Queen Mary once saw her staff eating with fish knives and forks and pronounced them unacceptable. If eating sole, for example, you hold the fish with one fork and pull the flesh away from the bone with the other - not as difficult as it sounds!

Soup

Soup should be served with a large serving spoon, which can be tipped gently into the mouth from the edge.

Side plates

These should be put on the left-hand side of the mat. Unless you have a very small knife which may be put on the plate, a small knife should be laid inside the sweet spoon.

Napkins

Napkins should not be put on the side plate but above and just to the left of the mat. This is the formal practice. I think it is quite acceptable to put the napkin on the mat or even on top of the plate if you have one on the table for the first course.

Asparagus

Many people eat asparagus with their fingers; therefore the table should be laid with finger bowls. These should contain a slice of lemon, which helps to take the grease off the fingers. There are now asparagus tongs; these can be put on the right-hand side of the mat on the outside.

Lobsters

Today there are lobster picks and crackers. Should you have neither of these (as I don't), make sure that the lobster claws are cracked and then put back into their shells or served without them, and the body of the lobster should have been pulled from its shell so that it only requires cutting. Finger bowls are advisable here too.

Pasta

In England it is correct to serve pasta with a large knife and fork. I serve it the Italian way, with a spoon and fork.

Cold Meats

If you are serving cold meats with a salad and also a HOT vegetable, then the hot vegetable should be served on a side plate that has been warmed.

Salt and Pepper

If possible, there should be one salt and pepper set between two people. If not, put them where they are easily accessible to several people.

Wine

Red wine should be decanted and white wine should be served cold from the bottle. Both should be put in coasters.

Desserts, Sweets and Puddings

Here we have instant confusion! In England, a dessert spoon and fork are what are used when eating fruit. A sweet is something like a crême brulée or bombe surprise or sweet pancakes. Puddings are served mainly at lunchtime and are usually baked, like treacle pudding, 'spotted dick', sponge and hot marmalade pudding. This is difficult for Americans and others as the world knows only the word dessert.

Toothpicks

These are a traditional addition to a dining table. They should be made of French quill and come from H.L. Jaccaz & Co. and can be bought in London at Harrods. They can be put in little silver boxes or stood upright in a little silver or glass pot.

Ashtrays

This is a highly controversial subject. These should be put directly above each place setting if they are small, or put on the table near the person smoking, preferably after people have finished eating.

There are lots of very chic and pretty ways of laying tables that bear no resemblance to the above. If you feel creative, follow your instincts and do whatever you want. I think that very few people remember what a table looks like unless it is especially beautiful or particularly bad. The most memorable table I ever sat at was probably the one done in the American Ambassador's Residence in London by Mrs Walter Annenberg. I remember that the table centres were grapes dipped in sugar mixed with white flowers, sitting in wonderful silver epergnes. They glowed in the candlelight. The silver was exquisite and the table linen - out of this world!

THE RECIPES

SPAGHETTI WITH ANCHOVIES AND PARSLEY

Simple spaghetti is delicious. This dish is quick and easy, and I usually serve it with a green salad. As the anchovies are very salty, it is better with gentle lettuce than iceberg, and with a slightly sweet dressing.

8 oz. fresh spaghetti
1 large bunch of chopped parsley (not too finely chopped)
crushed large clove of garlic
6 fillets of anchovy cut into small pieces
black pepper
olive oil

Cook the spaghetti in boiling water for 3 mins. and drain. Pour a little olive oil into the pan and stir so that all the pasta is coated with it. Then stir in the garlic, anchovies and fresh chopped parsley. Grind some black pepper over it and serve.

Serves 2

AVOCADO SOUP

Not original but much enjoyed by everyone I have given it to.

2 ripe avocadoes
1 teaspoon curry paste
¼ pt. single cream
1 pt. vegetable stock
juice of ½ lemon
salt and pepper
2 sprigs of parsley
2 sprigs of basil

Peel and chop the avocadoes and put into the blender with the curry paste, lemon juice, salt and pepper. Blend and then add cream.
Mix well.

Bring stock to the boil and then take off the heat. Add the avocado mixture slowly and reheat to serving temperature. Chop parsley and basil finely, and sprinkle on soup just before serving.

Serves 4

SHALLOTS COOKED WITH **BAY LEAVES**

The Italians serve this hot and cold; I prefer it hot
with either lamb or liver.

1½ lbs. of shallots
½ bottle of dry white wine
½ pint tomato sauce
1 handful bay leaves
chopped parsley
2 tablespoons of olive oil
salt and pepper

Fry the shallots in olive oil until golden. Put into
a greased baking dish with the wine, parsley, bay
leaves, stock and salt and pepper. Stir and then
cook in a medium oven until soft. Add water
if liquid evaporates before shallots are cooked.

Serves 6

CAULIFLOWER BALLS WITH PRAWNS

This is a very glamorous starter and is very easy to make. It looks better if it is served surrounded by either *mâche* (lamb's lettuce) or rocket. Use a large serving platter, preferably white.

2 large cauliflowers
1 pt. thick mayonnaise
1½ lbs. large prawns
2 pkts. rocket or mâche
1 lemon

Cut the leaves off the cauliflowers and see to it that they have a flat bottom. Either steam or boil them until just soft. MOST IMPORTANT: run them under cold water to refresh them. Pour over juice of 1 lemon. Leave until absolutely cold.

Smoothe mayonnaise over the cauliflowers and then cover them with the prawns, putting them as close to each other as possible, so that they look like pink balls. Place on serving dish and surround with rocket.

Serves 6

BREAD AND BUTTER
PUDDING

This recipe comes from Wiltons, 55 Jermyn Street, purveyor of fine Oysters, Fish and Game, one of the oldest and grandest restaurants in London. It dates back to 1742 and is particularly famous for good old-fashioned English recipes. This is one that people come from all over the world to enjoy.

10 slices of thick white bread
½ pt. milk
½ pt. double cream
4 oz. sultanas
3 eggs
½ teaspoon grated nutmeg
1 oz. butter
castor sugar
apricot glaze

Cut off all the crusts from the bread and cut each slice in half diagonally. Butter the bread and dip the buttered side into the sugar. Crack the eggs into a bowl, whisk slightly and then add the milk, cream and grated nutmeg. Place 5 slices of bread (butter side up) so they slightly overlap on the bottom of a small ovenproof dish and sprinkle with half the sultanas. Repeat a second layer with the remainder of the sultanas and cover with the mixture of eggs, milk and cream. Place the dish in a *bain-marie* of hot water to halfway, put into a high oven and cook for ½ hr. Finish off by brushing on the apricot glaze.

Serves 4

GALANTINE OF **CHICKEN** AND **HAM** WITH SAUCE VERTE SERVED WITH POTATOES VINAIGRETTE

This is much easier than it sounds and looks as if you have taken a lot of trouble. It is better if you make it a day in advance and leave it in the fridge overnight. I think it looks very attractive if you serve potatoes on the same dish.

10 skinless chicken breasts
8 slices of thick-cut lean ham
1½ sachets of gelatine
parsley
juice of ½ lemon
small glass of sherry
two 8-oz. tins of consommé
10 large baking potatoes
2 spring onions
vinaigrette made with grainy mustard

Fill a mug half-full with hot water. Pour the gelatine into it and stir well; leave until the gelatine is dissolved and liquid is cool. Chop chicken and ham into small pieces. Pour the consommé into a mixing bowl, add the gelatine, sherry, lemon juice and a little pepper, and stir gently.

Grease an 8 in. bread tin and put the chopped chicken and ham into it. Mix in the chopped parsley, making sure that some sticks to the bottom. Slowly pour on enough of the liquid mixture to cover and leave in the fridge overnight.

Peel potatoes and scoop them out into balls. Boil in salted water until soft but not mushy, then leave to cool. Chop spring onions very finely and mix together with the potatoes. Turn out the tin containing the chicken and ham mixture onto a large serving plate and, having poured vinaigrette over the potatoes, place them around the galantine.

I make sauce verte from ½ pt. mayonnaise blended with either 4 oz. of watercress or 4 oz. of spinach. Serve on the side.

Serves 8

GRILLED HARD-BOILED **EGGS** FILLED WITH **GOAT CHEESE**

A suitable dish as a starter for dinner in the summer. I worry about it a little, as quite a few people do not like goat cheese. This is a dish made by presentation: use a green dish or a glass one. Serve with hot herb or garlic bread.

6 hard-boiled eggs
6 oz. soft goat cheese
chives
rocket
black olives
vinaigrette

Cut hard-boiled eggs in half. Mash the yolk and mix with goat cheese. Add finely chopped chives and heap onto the eggs. Put under a hot grill until just brown. Serve surrounded with rocket tossed in vinaigrette. Sprinkle the black olives onto the rocket.

Serves 6

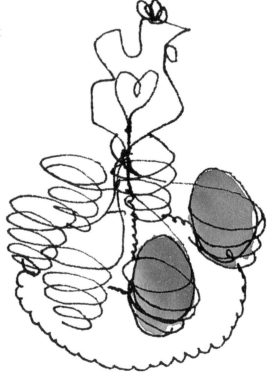

VEGETABLE CURRY

This is something I eat most weekends in the winter. There are endless permutations. Just use what you like on the vegetable counter but make a good mixture between root and green vegetables. Always remember that the root vegetables take longer to cook than the green, so sometimes it is better to start by cooking them and adding the green vegetables later. This is a typical example:

4 leeks
4 parsnips
4 carrots
4 potatoes
4 onions
4 cloves of garlic
4 tomatoes
6 oz. sliced green beans
1 tin of flageolet beans
1 vegetable stock cube
2 heaped teaspoons of hot curry paste
3 tablespoons of vegetable oil
salt and pepper

Chop all the vegetables. Put vegetable oil, garlic, chopped onions and curry paste into a frying pan and fry until soft. Add stock cube to a pt. of boiling water and stir until mixed. Put all the vegetables into a casserole, add the onions and the curry paste and cover with stock. Simmer in a medium oven for 1½ hrs. Taste, and if it is not hot enough for your taste, add more curry paste. Take out of the oven and allow to sit for at least 2 hrs.

When you want to serve it, put it back into the oven for 45 mins. and serve with lots of different chutneys and either garlic bread or baked potatoes.

Serves 8

SHIRLEY CONRAN'S
WARM BEAN SALAD

I had this delicious dish when staying with Shirley in her lovely house near Bordeaux. Here it is as she wrote it.

'This most adaptable and obliging recipe can be served as a starter (I like serving a vegetable alone as a starter) or as that part of the meal that fills what Katharine Whitehorn once called 'the potato-shaped gap'. Any leftovers will keep for 24 hours and are equally delicious served cold, though the taste is subtly different.

Ingredients:

½ cup of vegetable oil (not olive for it is too insistent a taste)
OR
½ cup of grainy mustard vinaigrette to which has been added ½ teaspoon of soy sauce
2 cloves chopped garlic
1 lb. dried white haricot beans soaked overnight or (if you believe that only anal-retentives remember to do so the night before) after breakfast for 8 hrs.
1 cup of black olives without stones
6 hard-boiled eggs, peeled
1 tablespoon of chopped parsley to garnish (optional but pretty)
salt and hand-ground black pepper

I keep a plastic bag of parsley in the deep freeze, hold it over the dish to be decorated and scrunch that part of the bag containing the parsley sprigs, which then flutter forth - thus I eliminate the chopping.

Boil the beans in salted water until *al dente*, not mushy. You may need to keep adding water until they are cooked. This may take up to 1½ hrs., depending on the beans.

Place the drained beans in a big salad bowl. Add all the other ingredients, the eggs having been sliced, and mix carefully with 2 wooden spoons. Sprinkle with parsley.'

Serves 8

Harry's Bar
VINAIGRETTE

This is the best there is. Made by Mario Cardani, the charming maître d' of this London restaurant club, it has to be the Rolls Royce version. He gave me his recipe, which unfortunately includes a couple of ingredients not many of us will have. I have made it at home with what I had and it is still superb. Harry's Bar serve this with a very light mixed green salad with slices of wonderful parmesan on it.

a pinch of sea salt
ground black pepper
1 teaspoon of Dijon mustard
1 dessertspoon of homemade wine vinegar
(5 years old)
3 dessertspoons of Cavalli (20-years-old
balsamic vinegar)
7 dessertspoons of olive oil

Put the salt in a bowl and then the two vinegars and whisk with a fork until the salt has dissolved. Slowly mix in the olive oil and lastly the black pepper.

I'm told that the first trace of the existence of balsamic vinegar appears in the year 1046 when Henry III, on the road to Rome to be crowned Emperor, made a request of Bonifacio, the Marquis of Tuscany in the vicinity of Piacenza, for a gift of a special vinegar that he had heard was made in the area. The region of Reggio Emilia is famous for growing the following grapes, Trebbiano, Occhio di Gatto, Spergola, Berzemino and Lambrusco. Traditional balsamic vinegar must be made within this area.

NOTE ON OLIVE OIL

This is the story of a cloud with a silver lining. I was driving home from work when my car was hit by a young man in a van. As my car was but a few weeks old, I was not very happy. The young man apologized, said it was entirely his fault and left looking very unhappy. Later that evening his employer, Charles Carey, of The Oil Merchant, 47 Ashcroft Grove, London, rang me to apologize for the accident and to say that he would happily rent me another car and pay for the damage to mine. I could not believe my ears!

Furthermore, he has sent me two wonderful bottles of virgin olive oils. Being curious, I asked him to tell me the difference between virgin and non-virgin oil. He tells me there are degrees of virginity!

EXTRA VIRGIN OIL implies that the olives have been picked by hand and taken off to the press to be crushed before they have had a chance to ferment. It must have less than 1% acidity.

'OLIVE OIL' is a blend of virgin oil and refined oil.

My new expert-friend tells me that Italian oils, especially those from Tuscany, are considered to be the best.

STRAWBERRIES
WITH **MINT**

Just a slight variation on a theme. I find the combination very tasty and refreshing.

2 lbs. of strawberries
bunch of young mint
icing sugar
double cream

Cut the strawberries in half. This is to let them absorb the flavour of the mint. Tear the mint leaves and mix them in with the strawberries. Cover with cling film and allow to sit for an hour. Put in a glass serving dish and sprinkle with icing sugar. Serve with double cream.

Serves 6

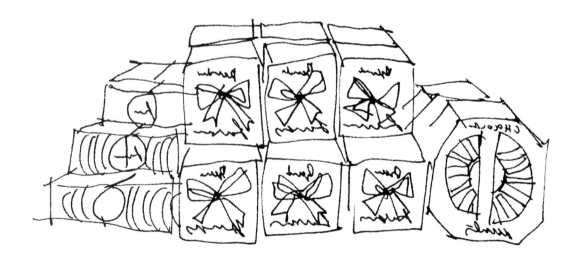

CHOCOLATE NUT
CRISPS

If you are a chocolate fan, you will find these hard to resist. They can be served with a soufflé or alongside a fruit fool, or just on their own after dinner.

6 oz. flaked almonds, toasted
1 cup castor sugar
½ cup water
2 oz. unsalted butter
6 oz. bitter cooking chocolate, melted
with a little water or milk

Put sugar and water into a pan. Stir over a low heat until the sugar dissolves. Caramelize by bringing to the boil until golden brown. This is best done in a non-stick pan, as it is easier to clean! Stir in the butter and remove from heat. Mix in the almonds and spoon onto some greased tinfoil making 1½ in. circles. Flatten with a knife. If the mixture becomes hard, return it to the heat for a few seconds. Allow to cool and then pour a little chocolate on the back of each one and refrigerate for ½ hr.

Serves 8

COLD PEA SOUP

This is not an original recipe but it is very useful in the summer. I sometimes serve it, rather like gazpacho, with a selection of very finely chopped vegetables.

1 peeled and finely chopped onion
1½ pts. chicken stock
1 lb. frozen peas
salt and pepper
2 teaspoons of sugar
finely chopped mint
4 tablespoons of creme fraiche

Put all ingredients except the creme fraiche into a pan and simmer for 5 mins. Cool, purée, adjust seasoning and chill. Add creme fraiche and stir well just before serving.

Serves 8

Curried **MUSHROOM**
SALAD

This is light, quick and pretty.

1 lb. of white button mushrooms
1 cup of Hellmann's mayonnaise
1 teaspoon curry paste
chopped chives
juice of ½ lemon
salt and ground black pepper
1 bunch of watercress

Wipe and slice the mushrooms thinly. Put in a mixing bowl and cover with the lemon juice. Add a pinch of salt and some black pepper. Mix the mayonnaise with the curry paste and fold into the mushrooms.

Put into the centre of a flat serving dish, surround with watercress and sprinkle with the chopped chives. Serve with hot French bread.

Serves 6

BLENHEIM BOMBE

The Duke and Duchess of Marlborough have very kindly given me the two following recipes. The food at Blenheim Palace is exquisite and very creative. Even though the kitchens are a long way from the dining room, they produce the most wonderful cuisine.

The easy way to make this dish is to buy a good quality ready-made ice cream. However, if you are going to make your own ice cream, the recipe is as follows.

For the ice cream:

6 egg yolks
7.5 fl. oz. double cream
7.5 fl. oz. milk
4 oz. castor sugar
vanilla pod (halved lengthways, and with the seeds scraped out)

Place the egg yolks in a metal bowl. Boil the milk and cream together with the vanilla pod. Sieve on to the egg yolks while whisking vigorously. Add the castor sugar and whisk in. You can add a little more sugar if you prefer your ice cream sweeter.

Place the bowl over a pan of boiling water and whisk the mixture until it thickens just enough to coat the back of a spoon. Freeze the mixture down either in an ice cream machine, or by placing in the freezer and stirring occasionally.

Place individual dariol moulds in the freezer and when very cold line with the ice cream, pressing it well into the corners with a teaspoon and leaving a hole in the middle. Allow to re-freeze. Fill the centre with either grated chocolate or crumbled Cadbury's 'Flake'.

To serve:

Dip briefly into hot water and turn out onto a chilled plate.

Blenheim Bombe is normally served with hot chocolate sauce. A good quick 'fun' recipe for this is simply to melt gently 2 or 3 Mars bars with a splash of milk, taking care to stir continually and not let it get too hot or burn. Serve with the bombes on the side.

Serves 8

FILLETS OF **SOLE** WITH SAFFRON MAYONNAISE AND FRESH HERBS

12 quarter fillets of sole
4 shallots
½ oz. chopped parsley
½ oz. fresh basil leaves
½ oz. fresh chervil leaves
sprig of fresh thyme
pinch of ground saffron
¼ glass white wine
salt and pepper
½ cup mayonnaise
olive oil

Wash and trim the sole. Chop the shallots very finely. Remove the leaves from the thyme. Put a light smear of oil on the bottom of the dish you are cooking the fish in. Put a layer of fish down. Moisten with wine and a light thread of olive oil. Sprinkle with salt and pepper, a few thyme leaves and a little saffron. Repeat until all the fish is used and cover with greaseproof paper. Place in a very hot oven and cook until just done. This will not take very long, approx. 10 mins.

When cooked, remove the fillets and place on a cooling rack. Reduce the liquid until syrupy. Mix this with mayonnaise to taste. Mix all the herbs together, having chopped them.

Take the cooked fish and dip in the mayonnaise mixture one fillet at a time and place on a serving dish. Sprinkle with fresh herbs and a light thread of good olive oil.

Serves 4

FOCCACCIA WITH HAM AND CHEESE

This is an ideal lunch dish for 4 ladies. It takes very little time and is very good. Serve with a salad.

1 round foccaccia loaf
¼ lb. of very thin ham cut into strips
¼ lb. parmesan sliced
¼ lb. mature cheddar sliced
¼ lb. gruyere sliced
black pepper
moutarde de Meaux

Cut the top off the foccaccia, leaving ⅔ on the bottom, and scoop out the inside. Put in a layer of mixed cheeses and a layer of ham, and sprinkle with black pepper. Repeat until all the ingredients are used. The filling should be higher than the sides of the bottom layer.

Cover the inside of the foccaccia top with the mustard and press down over the filling. Wrap in tin foil and bake in a hot oven for 20 mins. Then uncover the top and bake for a further 5 mins. Remove from the tin foil and serve with a salad.

Serves 4

BEETROOT PASTA

A wonderful summertime lunch dish or a starter. There is something very appealing about pink pasta; I serve this on a large round white plate.

1 packet of angel hair pasta or spaghettini
6 medium-sized beetroots cooked
1 bunch of spring onions
1 bunch of chives
1 large cup of mustard vinaigrette
ground black pepper

Cook the pasta as directed on the packet and rinse. Leave to cool. Chop the beetroot into small squares and put into a bowl. Cover with the vinaigrette and some black pepper. Stir well and then mix with the pasta. Chop the spring onions and mix them in. Put on to a serving plate and at the last moment sprinkle with chopped chives.

Serves 8

LOKSHEN KUGEL

Jonathan and Thalia Stone came to lunch with me one day and we were talking about this book. He asked if I had included any kosher recipes. Very ashamed, I said that I had not. He then sent me the following, which is delicious. Here it is as he sent it to me:

A generation ago, this dish was made every Friday and cooked overnight for serving hot on Saturday. It is a good-tempered dish that can be cooked at the most convenient temperature without detriment. To achieve the crust lining which is the best part of the kugel, the fat is first heated in the cooking dish, then swirled round the sides to coat them.

4 oz. broad egg noodles (Lokshen)
1 egg
a pinch each of cinnamon and salt
grated rind of ½ lemon
2 oz. sugar
1 oz. margarine
2 tablespoons of currants

Set the oven to 190°C, put the margarine into a 2-in. deep oven casserole and place in the oven. Meanwhile, boil the noodles according to packet directions, then put into a sieve and rinse with cold water to remove excess starch. Drain well.

Whisk the egg and sugar, then stir in the flavourings and the currants. Finally, stir in the noodles and the hot fat which has been swirled round the baking dish. Bake for 45 mins. or until set with a crisp brown top.

Serves 4

PRAWN AND RICE TIMBALE

One can make this some time before it is required. I use it as a starter for a dinner party or for a summer 'ladies lunch'. You can decorate it with all sorts of different things, such as cold asparagus or samphire.

6 oz. of basmati rice
8 oz. of peeled prawns
⅓ of a cucumber
3-4 spring onions
2 tablespoons of chopped parsley
half a mug of vinaigrette made with grainy mustard
1 pkt. of rocket
¼ pt. mayonnaise

Boil the rice in plenty of water for 10 mins., drain and refresh with cold water, then drain again. Mix the prawns with chopped cucumber, chopped spring onions and chopped parsley. Add the rice when cold and mix with vinaigrette.

Put into a circular, slightly greased ring mould and leave in the fridge for a least 2 hrs. Turn out onto a serving plate and fill the centre with rocket. Serve with mayonnaise on the side and some hot herb bread.

Serves 6

LEEK AND SALMON
FISHCAKES

This is really an ideal way to use leftover leeks and potatoes, but I will give the recipe from scratch. Excellent for Sunday night, or whenever you feel like comfort food. The result is more like 'bubble and squeak' than fishcakes.

6 large potatoes mashed
4 leeks
vegetable oil
2 salmon steaks
salt and pepper

Slice the leeks into circles and sauté until soft. Leave to cool. Make (or buy) mashed potatoes and allow to cool. Poach salmon and take off the bone. Mix all ingredients in a mixing bowl without breaking up the fish or leeks too much. Pat into shape and fry in a non-stick pan, using only a little vegetable oil, until brown.

You can keep these hot in the oven for quite a time. Serve with either a tomato sauce or ketchup.

Serves 4

PENNE WITH YELLOW PEPPER COULIS

In this house there is never any excuse needed to eat pasta. This is a very pretty dish and very quick to make. You can make it several hours ahead, using either fresh or dried pasta, and serve it cold or serve it tiède.

500 g. of penne
3 yellow peppers
4 tablespoons of sunflower oil
salt and black pepper
chopped parsley

Cut 2 peppers and remove the seeds. Put them into the blender and blend until smooth. Take out and drain off excess liquid, leaving a thickish pulp. Cut the remaining pepper and take out the inside, then slice into bite-size pieces.

Put the blended pepper back into the machine with the oil, salt and pepper.

Cook the penne until *al dente*, rinse and place in a serving plate. Pour on the pepper coulis and then gently mix in the strips of pepper. Sprinkle with chopped parsley and serve.

Serves 6

WINE JELLY

This is an easy recipe and is very good at the end of a rich dinner. One can fill the mould with red fruit, but I think it is more chic served on its own with cheese straws.

1 bottle of house claret
1½ oz. of gelatine
1 cup of hot water
1 tablespoon of sugar

Pour the gelatine into the cup of hot water and stir until dissolved and clear. Allow to cool. Then mix with wine and pour into a ring mould. Allow to stand in the fridge overnight. To serve, lower the mould into a sink of hot water for a few seconds and then turn out onto the serving plate.

Serves 6

CURRIED PARSNIP SOUP

I love soups and will have them at any time. This is a good soup for winter evenings served with hot garlic bread or herb bread.

8 medium parsnips
2 large potatoes
1 large clove of garlic
1 large onion
1 tablespoon of chopped parsley
1½ pts. of vegetable stock
1 dessertspoon of curry paste
1 tablespoon of sunflower oil
salt and pepper

Peel and chop the parsnips, potatoes and onion. Put sunflower oil into a pan with shredded garlic and curry paste. Fry until the garlic is turning golden, then add the parsnips, potatoes and onion and a cup of stock. Simmer until the vegetables are soft and mushy. Add the remaining stock and simmer for 5 mins. Take off the heat and put through the blender, seasoning to taste. Add water if too thick.

Return to the pan and add the chopped parsley.

Serves 8

WHITE SPAGHETTI

There must be a proper name for this. It is my favourite way of eating spaghetti and I think it is very healthy.

1 pkt. spaghetti
2 cloves of garlic chopped roughly
1 VERY FINELY chopped red chilli with no seeds
½ cup olive oil
salt
grated parmesan

Cook the spaghetti in boiling salted water until *al dente*. In the meantime fry the garlic in a little oil. Put the spaghetti back in the pan it was cooked in with the garlic, chilli and all the oil. Toss well and reheat for 2 mins.

Serves 6

Stuffed **ONIONS**

This does not take long to make and is rather original. It is a good lunch dish or alternatively a starter for dinner.

8 large onions
1 lb. sage and pork stuffing
1 cup fine breadcrumbs
olive oil
½ pt. spicy tomato sauce
basil

Peel the onions and slice off the bottom so that they will sit upright. Boil until tender. Cut the tops off and allow to cool.

Scoop out the centre of the onions and fill with sausage meat stuffing. Pat breadcrumbs on the top and pour a little olive oil over each one. Place in a greased serving dish and bake for 45 mins. in a medium oven (350°F). Remove and serve with a hot spicy tomato sauce with plenty of shredded basil in it.

Serves 8

GOAT CHEESE
SANDWICH

I found this in Israel with Mr and Mrs Max
Fisher when staying in the King David Hotel.
We all thought it was delicious, and it makes a
good lunch dish.

loaf of challah bread
1 large aubergine
6 oz. of soft goat cheese
3 plum tomatoes
pesto sauce
olive oil
salt and pepper

Slice the aubergine and lightly grease with olive
oil. Grill until just soft. Slice the tomatoes. Cut
the bread into $\frac{1}{2}$ in. slices and toast. Spread
with pesto sauce. Put 1 layer of aubergine and
1 layer of tomatoes on each slice, add salt and
pepper to taste. Slice the goat cheese into $\frac{1}{4}$
in. thick slices and put on top of tomatoes.
Place under a hot grill for a few minutes until
just browning. Serve immediately.

This dish could also have a few grilled peppers
in it.

Serves 6

PEA SALAD

This is a recipe from Marjorie Fisher; I've had it in her house and it is delicious. It makes a very good starter for lunch.

16 oz. petit pois lightly cooked and cooled
12 oz. tinned sweetcorn
1 bunch of spring onions chopped
1 green pepper finely chopped
one 4-oz. jar of red pimento drained and sliced
1 stick of celery chopped
1 large carrot grated
½ cup of wine vinegar
¼ cup of olive oil
½ cup of granulated sugar
1 teaspoon of celery salt
salt and pepper

Mix oil, vinegar, etc. and pour over the vegetables. Allow to sit overnight, and turn several times. Serve chilled.

Serves 10

SALMON WITH **PINK GINGER** ON A BED OF **SPINACH**

I was introduced to pink ginger, or for that matter any ginger, by Anouska Hempel. She is one of the women I admire most in the world for her originality and her stubborn determination to achieve perfection. This is not one of her recipes but it was inspired by her.

6 boneless salmon pieces
2 tablespoons of Japanese sushi ginger
olive oil
salt and pepper
2 lbs. of fresh spinach

Grease a small ovenproof dish and place the salmon pieces on it. Sprinkle with salt and pepper. Cover with slices of pink ginger. Cook for 10 mins. in a medium oven.

Cook the spinach in boiling water until tender. Drain and place under the salmon pieces. This dish can be served tiède, and hollandaise sauce on the side is an excellent accompaniment.

Serves 6

Mixed **CRUDITÉ** PLATTER

This is one of my favourite starters, either for a summer meal or for a Sunday lunch if I feel that whatever I am making as a main course needs finishing off. Use a large round or rectangular plate, as you will need to put a bowl of houmous in the middle.

8 oz. black olives *de Provence*
8 oz. houmous
8 oz. carrot batons
1 bunch of spring onions
1 box of cherry tomatoes
24 hard-boiled quail's eggs
12 slices of pepper salami
1 head of green celery cut into 3-in. strips

Put the houmus into a small bowl in the centre of a large white plate, preferably round. Lay out all the other ingredients around it, taking care with the colours.

Garlic or herb bread with olive oil are very suitable with this.

Serves 10

Rolled Stuffed Omelet

This is my version of an Italian recipe. It is very good served with a green salad. Being an omelet, it has to be finished and served fairly quickly, so it is better as a kitchen supper or lunch.

1 lb. leaf spinach
½ cup parmesan cheese
2 hard-boiled eggs chopped
1 clove of garlic
6 eggs, beaten
salt and pepper
olive oil

Put finely sliced garlic in a pan with a little oil and fry until softened. Add spinach with some salt and pepper and simmer for 6 mins. I usually chop the spinach with scissors while it is cooking, as that makes it easier to cut the omelet.

Take off the heat and add chopped hard-boiled eggs, parmesan and a tablespoon of oil. Heat a non-stick frying pan with a little oil and pour in the beaten eggs. Cook until almost set. Slide the omelet onto a large plate and spread the spinach mixture on it. Roll up and place on a greased baking dish and put into oven at 400°F or 200°C for 5 mins. and serve.

Serves 4

Broad beans, caper, anchovy and **Bacon** salad

This is one of the best and easiest salads I have ever eaten. I had it In France at an elegant lunch given by Virginia and Peter Blond. There was a certain amount of discussion around the table as to the origin of the recipe, but there was not a bean left on any plate!

2 lbs. of broad beans, either frozen or fresh
2 teaspoons of small capers
10 anchovy fillets cut small
6 hard-boiled eggs sliced
8 rashers of crispy thin streaky bacon
1 cup of sweet vinaigrette

Cook the broad beans until just soft. Rinse in cold water and drain. Leave to cool. When cool put out on a flat serving dish. Mix in the anchovies and capers, and place slices of egg on the top. Pour on the vinaigrette and mix lightly. Sprinkle the bacon over the top.

Serves 8

CURRIED **MELON**
BALLS (recipe on p. 65)

COD WITH **CHILLI** AND SHREDDED **COURGETTES** (recipe on p. 73)

BEETROOT TERRINE
WITH SOUR CREAM AND CHIVES

This is a good starter at any time of year and looks pretty. This is a dish I designed for the US Ambassador Charles and Mrs Price because she liked beetroots and England.

1 lb. of cooked small beets
2 sachets of gelatine
salt and pepper
juice of ½ lemon and zest
2 tablespoons of balsamic vinegar
sour cream
chives

Chop the beets finely. Mix the gelatine with ½ pt. of warm water. Add the lemon juice and zest. When cool, add seasoning and vinegar, pour over the beetroot and stir. Put into an 8-in. rectangular mould and leave in the fridge for 4 hrs.

To turn out, dip the bottom of the mould in hot water, cover with a plate and turn upside down. Cut in slices and serve with sour cream and chives on the side.

Serves 4

PRUNE SOUFFLÉ

This is an unfailing winner. It is not a real soufflé, but it looks and tastes delicious. It is also much less likely to fall on its face between the kitchen and the dining room!

3 tins of prunes in syrup
10 egg whites
1 tablespoon of castor sugar
juice of ½ lemon

Take the prunes out of two tins and drain off the juice. Put on one side. After removing the stones, put the prunes in the blender.

Butter a soufflé dish for 8 servings. Beat egg whites until they are stiff and will stand up in peaks. Fold in the sugar. Then fold in the pureed prunes, using a metal spoon. Put the mixture into the soufflé dish, piling it quite high or at least to the very top of the dish, and put in a hot oven for ½ hr.

For the sauce, drain the last tin of prunes, take out the stones and puree. Add the lemon juice and serve with the soufflé.

Serves 8

Scallops
WITH GREEN THAI CURRY

This recipe was given to be by my friend Bhupen Takker. He serves the scallops on a bed of crisps and I have changed that to a bed of Chinese seaweed which you can buy already shredded and just heat up.

12 scallops
1 tablespoon of Thai green curry paste
4 tablespoons of hazelnut oil
1 bunch of spring onions for garnish
2 pkts. of Chinese crispy seaweed

Heat the oil and fry the curry paste for a couple of minutes, ensuring that it merges with the oil. Add scallops and cook quickly.

Follow instructions on how long to heat the seaweed. Put it onto a serving dish when heated and place the scallops on top. Pour the curry juice over the scallops. Cut the spring onions into long thin strips and place them around the dish.

Serves 4

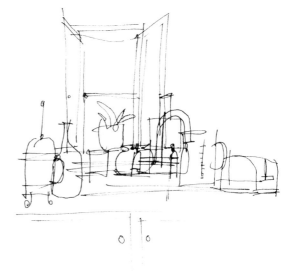

MOZZARELLA AND SALAMI SALAD

Quick and easy. I offer this when I have a vision of a good main course that I want to spend a bit of time on.

2 pkts. buffalo mozzarella
2 pkts. various salamis
vinaigrette
1 pkt. croutons
black olives
mustard vinaigrette

Dice mozzarella into cubes. Make a small amount of vinaigrette with grainy mustard. Lay salamis out on a dish in alternate arrangement of flavours. Mix vinaigrette with croutons and mozzarella. Place in the centre of serving dish. Sprinkle on black olives and serve with hot bread.

Serves 4

CRABMEAT AND CELERY SALAD

This can either be served as a first course or, in warmer weather, as a main course. One can also make it grander by using white crab meat, but I normally use dressed crab from one of the supermarkets. It looks very pretty served in scallop shells.

4 dressed crabs
2 tablespoons of Hellmann's mayonnaise
juice of ½ lemon
5 small celery hearts
black pepper
2 pkts. of chives

Put the crab in a bowl and mix in the lemon, mayonnaise and black pepper. Chop the celery into pieces about ½ in. thick and add to the mixture. It will then be slightly pinkish from the brown meat of the crab.

Put either into scallop shells or onto a serving dish and sprinkle liberally with chopped chives.

Serves 6

MICHAEL WATSON'S
DUCK

My good friend Michael Watson is a very elegant host and a superb cook. I am setting down this recipe exactly as he gave it to me; his English is as lovely as his cooking.

To roast duck whole ensures that if the breast is 'done to a turn', the legs will still be raw - and to cook them separately is tedious. Added to which, it's my experience that even after the most expert carving one is left with depressingly little to eat. The solution today is to buy duck breasts on their own - preferably those that have not been frozen - and they are increasingly easy to find. (You need 1 per person and they usually come 2 in a pack.)

Some hold that the best way to roast duck is very, very slowly but in my experience the result is invariably disappointing and the skin will be flabby. Much better, and easier, is to cook FAST.

Preheat the oven to 200°C/400°F. Lightly smear with olive oil the surface of a standard oven dish (26 x 34 cms), which will hold 6 duck breasts. Trim the excess fat from the breasts with scissors, but be sure to leave enough skin to cover the meat. Now pat the breasts dry with paper towels and place them in the dish. Next, give them a generous sprinkling of salt. (If you are worried about salt intake, don't be. While roasting, most of the salt will be drawn off with the fat.)

Put the breasts into the oven for 25 mins. In the process they will shrink somewhat and at the end the skin will have turned in colour from a liverish white to a crisp golden brown. The colour of the skin will determine whether they are ready to serve or require a minute or two more.

As for accompaniments, you can't improve on segments of orange in a sweetish French dressing, well-flavoured with garlic, mashed potatoes rather than roast, and well-minted green peas.

Serves 6

KUMQUAT MARMALADE

- another Michael Watson 'special'. I did not invent this recipe. It came to me from Australia where kumquats thrive, along with all other citrus fruits. This enables me to say that if you follow the recipe slavishly, the result will be spectacular. Attempt to modify it (as I did initially) and it won't be as good.

4½ lbs. (2 kilograms) kumquats
10 cups of cold water
10 cups of sugar
whisky

Slice kumquats into strips and at the same time remove the pips. Pour on the water and leave overnight. Next day bring the mixture to the boil and then simmer until the liquid runs clear. Set aside for 24 hrs.

Now bring to the boil again, remove from the heat and add the sugar. Stir until the sugar is dissolved. Reboil for 35 mins. Then, for every pound of sliced fruit that you began with, add a modest dessertspoonful of whisky. Stir and bottle at once.

QUAIL WITH MARMALADE AND MUSTARD

Quail are delicious hot or cold, and this recipe can be eaten either way. If you serve it cold, I suggest that it be accompanied by a chopped beetroot salad and mashed potatoes. Served hot it is good with small roast parsnips and a herbed purée of potatoes.

8 quail
soya sauce
½ jar of runny orange marmalade
2 tablespoons of Thai chilli dipping sauce
2 tablespoons of grainy mustard
½ cup of dry white wine
8 small parsnips
6 large white potatoes
parsley
basil
chives
olive oil
butter
salt and pepper

Marinate quail with some soya sauce, Thai chilli dipping sauce and a little olive oil.

Slice parsnips in half and put in a serving dish in the oven with 2 tablespoons of olive oil and a knob of butter. Cook in a hot oven for 45 mins., turning occasionally.

Boil the potatoes and mash them with a little olive oil. Season to taste. Add the chopped herbs and keep hot until the quail and parsnips are cooked.

Mix the marmalade and mustard. Place quail on a greased baking dish and cover with the mixture. Add white wine. Cook in a hot oven for 30 mins. Stir juices and serve.

Serves 4

HADDOCK, TURMERIC
AND **SPINACH** SOUP

This is really more than a soup. It is a fish dish.
You can use it as a main course, just served with
mashed potatoes on the side, or as a starter with
hot herb bread.

1 lb. smoked haddock fillet
½ pt. milk
½ pt. fish stock
¼ pt. double cream
½ lb. fresh spinach, chopped
small teaspoonful of turmeric
salt and black pepper

Put the milk and stock into a pan with the
haddock, and simmer until the haddock is flaky.
Take off the heat and remove the haddock. Take
off the skin and flake into bite-size pieces.

Bring the liquid to the boil, having added the
cream, black pepper, turmeric and salt to taste.
Take off the heat while you add the fish and the
spinach, and serve as soon as it is hot through.

Serves 4

Leeks
WITH **FETA CHEESE**
AND CHILLI VINAIGRETTE

I think of this as an autumn dish, as leeks are more available then. It is a useful starter for Sunday lunch or as a supper dish.

8 large leeks
6 oz. feta cheese
vinaigrette made with drop of chilli oil

Slice the leeks into small rings and blanch in boiling water for 3 mins. Drain and allow to cool. Make the vinaigrette using chilli oil. Put the leeks onto a serving dish and sprinkle with crumbled feta cheese. Pour on the vinaigrette and leave to sit for ½ hr. before serving.

Serves 6

Sultana ASPIC

When you are serving either foie gras or terrines this is a very good extra. It is quite delicious, looks rather sophisticated, and takes no time to make.

6 oz. of juicy sultanas
1 sachet of gelatine
small glass of white wine

Put the gelatine into ½ pt. hot water and stir until dissolved. Add white wine. When cool, pour this liquid over the sultanas in a shallow non-stick baking tray. Put into the fridge for 4 hrs. or until set. To turn out, dip the dish in hot water and then turn onto a flat surface. Cut the aspic into 2-in. diamonds. Serve beside the foie gras.

Serves 8

TOMATO BRUSCHETTA

A delicious starter than can be made the day before and kept in the fridge.

6 large ripe beefsteak tomatoes
3 cloves of garlic
4 oz. virgin olive oil
bunch of basil
salt and pepper
loaf of ciabatta bread

Chop the tomatoes into a pulp. I do this with kitchen scissors in a bowl. Crush the garlic and mix in with the tomatoes. Add olive oil, salt and pepper, and put into the fridge for several hours.

Remove from the fridge and drain excess liquid. Slice the bread and toast under the grill. Put large spoonfuls of the tomato mixture onto each slice of toast and serve with a sprig of basil on top. This looks at its best served on a plain white plate.

Serves 6

HADDOCK MONTE CARLO

A very famous dish in a good fish restaurant. This does not detract from its charm. I love it!

1 lb. of smoked haddock
1 pt. of milk
1 bay leaf
2 oz. butter
2 oz. plain flour
salt and pepper
1 teaspoon tomato paste
4 oz. grated mature cheddar cheese
4 soft poached eggs

Cut the haddock into 4 pieces and poach in milk with the bay leaf for about 5 mins. Remove skin. Use the milk to make a cheese sauce. Add tomato paste.

Put the eggs on top of the haddock and then pour the sauce over them. Place under a hot grill for 2-3 mins. and serve.

Serves 4

DUCK WITH WATER CHESTNUTS AND GREEN PEPPERCORNS

Michael Watson thinks duck should be cooked very quickly. This recipe requires the opposite. The duck breasts remain very tender and pink if they are cooked very slowly. Serve with gratiné potatoes and a purée of spinach.

8 duck breasts
2 tins of water chestnuts
1 jar of soft green peppercorns in brine
2 tablespoons of light oil
1 glass of white wine
soya sauce
2 tablespoons of black peppercorns
4 bay leaves
2 cloves of garlic sliced

Sauce:

1 pt. orange juice
1 chicken stock cube dissolved in ½ cup
hot water
one 6 oz. jar of red currant jelly
black pepper
juice of ½ lemon

Put duck breasts in a dish and cover with oil, 1 tablespoon of soya sauce, white wine, black peppercorns, bay leaves and garlic. Cover and leave to marinate for several hours. Cook in medium oven for about ½ hr. covered with tin foil until duck breasts are just cooked.

Remove from oven, allow to cool. Remove skin and fat, and leave the duck breasts sitting in their juices.

Put all ingredients for the sauce into a pan and boil. Reduce the sauce until it is quite thick and shiny.

Place the duck breasts in a serving dish and, having drained the water chestnuts and green peppercorns, put them around the duck. Cover with the sauce and return to a very low oven for about ½ hr. to heat through.

Serves 8

SPINACH RAMEKINS

This is not only delicious, but very quick and easy
to make. It also looks much more difficult
than it is.

2 pkts. frozen chopped spinach
1 large onion, chopped very finely
8 oz. Philadelphia cream cheese
1 tin of consommé
salt and black pepper

Defrost the spinach and put in a pan. Heat until
all the liquid has gone. Add the cream cheese,
salt and a generous amount of black pepper and
stir until the cheese is soft and creamy. Take off
the heat and add the onion. Put into ramekin
dishes, leaving enough room for ½ in.
consommé on the top. Chill for at least 2 hrs. and
then pour on the consommé.

Leave in the fridge until jelly has set. Serve with
hot French or garlic bread.

Serves 10

CURRIED **MELON**
BALLS

Kenneth J. Lane, the most famous and talented designer of costume jewelry, the best host in New York, likes curried melon balls. He is one of the most perfect guests I have ever had to stay and will eat anything!

3 melons, 1 pink-fleshed, 1 green and 1 yellow
½ pt. light mayonnaise
1 heaped teaspoon of hot curry paste
chives

Chill the melons and then make balls out of the flesh. Mix the curry paste in with the mayonnaise and toss with the melon balls. Sprinkle chopped chives over the top and serve with hot herb bread.

Serves 8

GRAPE DESSERT

This recipe is very easy to prepare. The trick is to make it look better than it actually is by putting it into a very attractive dish. The last time I made it I used a beautiful Lalique bowl with a gold rim.

2½ lbs. of red and green seedless grapes
½ lemon
heavy cream or sorbet

Just cut the grapes in half, place them in the dish and squeeze the lemon over the top. Serve with either double cream or a sorbet of a matching colour and THERE YOU HAVE IT!

Serves 8

BEETROOT MASHED POTATOES

As a lover of bright colours, I find this very appealing. I use it as a base for darker coloured meats and also for chicken served with mushrooms. It can also be served just as a vegetable on its own.

Make 1½ lbs. of mashed potatoes
1 lb. cooked beetroot chopped into small squares
½ cup olive oil
¼ cup vinegar
1 teaspoon mustard
salt and pepper

Make a vinaigrette of the mustard, olive oil, vinegar, salt and pepper. Mix the mashed potatoes with the beetroot and fold in the vinaigrette. Heat and serve.

Serves 6

SAUSAGE MEAT LOAF

In most supermarkets you can buy large packets of sausage meat. I prefer the one flavoured with sage and onion. This dish is very quick to make and is good served with either fried or baked potatoes and a ratatouille.

3 lbs. sausage meat
4 hard-boiled eggs

Put the sausage meat on a greased sheet of tinfoil and flatten until about 1½ in. thick. Lay the hard-boiled eggs in a line down the middle. Roll the sausage meat round the eggs and close the tinfoil tightly around. Twist the ends closed.

You can now roll this until it is the shape required. Remove the tinfoil and place the loaf on a non-stick pan and cook in a hot oven for 1 hr. It is particularly good if it is slightly burnt, rather like burnt sausages.

It can be served cold with a green salad.

Serves 6

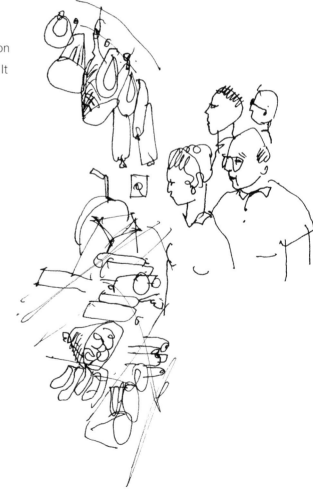

DRUNKEN **PINEAPPLE**

Jeremy and Mary James gave this to us on our
honeymoon! I think I have got the recipe right.
It should be given only to people with strong
heads.

2 ripe pineapples
¼ bottle of brandy
4 tablespoons of dark brown sugar
rind of 1 lemon
½ lb. butter

Peel and cut the pineapples into bite-size pieces.
Put in a frying pan with butter, brandy and lemon
peel. Add the dark brown sugar and simmer until
pineapple is tender and the juice has reduced to a
thick brown sauce - approx. 45 mins.

Serves 8

FISH STEW

This is 'to die for'! Very easy and very good for the figure!

10 oz. fillet of salmon
10 oz. fillet of cod or haddock
200 g. tiger prawns
4 sticks of celery
1 pkt. carrot sticks (200 g. diced carrots)
2 small onions
1 large clove of garlic
1 tin green flageolet beans (400 g.)
1 pkt. coriander
1 pt. vegetable stock
1 teaspoon of sweet chilli sauce
1 teaspoon of safflower oil

Sauté garlic in oil until soft. Chop onions and celery, and add to the pan along with carrots, flageolet beans and vegetable stock. Simmer until carrots are just tender. Cut fish into chunks and add with prawns and chilli sauce. Simmer until fish is cooked, then fold in chopped coriander. Serve with new or mashed potatoes.

Serves 6

JE NE SAIS PAS QUOI FRANÇAIS

Lord and Lady Swathling gave me this recipe in their lovely house Farat, near Toulouse. We ate it before lunch with a glass of muscat or before dinner with a glass of champagne. It is a sort of cake, made with eggs and ham and peppers, to be served with an apéritif. I can only give you the recipe exactly as it was given to me.

20 g. flour
6 eggs
2 large teaspoons of Dijon mustard
1 green pepper
1 red pepper
100 g. pitted black olives
100 g. pitted green olives
200 g. of lean ham
200 g. of parmesan cheese
salt and pepper

Put the mustard in a mixing bowl. Pour in the beaten eggs and mix thoroughly. Sprinkle in the flour and mix. Chop everything else and mix together. Put in a greased rectangular terrine dish and bake in the oven for 1 hr. and 5 mins. Allow to cool, turn out onto a serving dish and slice.

Serves 8

Salad pavlovsk

With his permission, I pass on this recipe of Kenny Lane's which can be made at a moment's notice any payday! It is perfect for an al fresco lunch in the garden.

18 baby russet potatoes
1 bottle of reasonably good champagne
(flat is OK)
as much Ossietra caviar as you can afford
½ cup of creme fraiche or heavy cream
½ lemon

Boil the potatoes in their skins. Slightly cool them so that your sous-chef does not burn his fingers. Skin and slice while still warm. Cover completely with champagne and allow to sit at room temperature for several hours while champagne is absorbed. Drain off excess champagne.

Add the caviar, sprinkle with lemon juice, add cream and gently toss. Devour with as much champagne, not flat, as you can afford.

Serves 8

COD WITH **CHILLI** AND SHREDDED **COURGETTES**

I invented this dish for my friends Booby Gelber and Emma Gibbs as they are always teasing me about not being able to eat very hot food. I am a chilli fan in moderation. This is a very easy recipe and takes very little time to prepare. It will not blow the roof off your mouth, but it is hot!

4 cod fillets approx. 5 ins. long
1 jar of medium hot chilli sauce
10 small courgettes
safflower oil
salt and pepper

Place the cod in greased tinfoil, add salt and pepper, and wrap. Poach in a little water in an oven at 350°F for about 7 mins. Take out and drain.

Chop the courgettes very finely and fry in a hot pan with a little oil until just soft. Place the fish in a serving dish, cover with entire jar of chilli sauce, surround with courgettes and place in a medium oven until warmed through.

Serves 4

STUFFED **ORANGE PEPPERS**

The colour of orange peppers has always fascinated me. They look very glamorous. This is a lunchtime dish for summer and can be prepared in advance. The longer it sits the more the mixture picks up the flavour of the pepper.

6 orange peppers
½ lb. cooked fusilli pasta
chopped chives
1 small tin of red pimentos, chopped finely
¼ pt. mayonnaise
1 crushed garlic clove
chopped parsley
black pepper
1 tablespoon tomato ketchup
basil

Cut the tops off the peppers and clean out the insides. Cut a thin slice off the bottom so that they all sit upright. Mix all the other ingredients together, fill the peppers and put back the tops. Chill for ½ hr. and serve with sprigs of basil.

Serves 6

GINGER BISCUIT
PUDDING

Making puddings is not my forte, and I happen not to have a sweet tooth myself, so every pudding recipe you get in this book is given somewhat reluctantly. I do know, however, that this one seems to go down a treat.

2 pkts. ginger biscuits
1 pt. whipping cream
grated rind of 2 oranges
6 oz. split almonds

Crush the ginger biscuits with a rolling pin, leaving them in small bits rather than complete crumbs. Whip the cream until it stays in points. Grate the orange rind and then mix all three ingredients together. Put in a glass dish in the fridge for several hours.

Serves 8

BABY AUBERGINES
WITH **CREAM CHEESE** AND **HAM**

Aubergines always look so wonderful when they are raw and lose a lot of their charm when cooked. Sadly, this recipe is no exception, so it is made to look attractive by the colour of the ham.

12 baby aubergines
1 large pkt. of Philadelphia cream cheese
8 oz. very thinly shredded boiled ham or Parma ham
olive oil
balsamic vinegar

Cook the aubergines whole in the microwave for approx. 4 mins. or until just soft. Allow to cool and then split them without removing the stalks. Fill the centres with cream cheese and add a little ham folded. Place on a serving dish and pour about ¼ cup each of olive oil and balsamic vinegar onto the plate. They will mix themselves into lovely designs.

Serves 6

CHICKEN TONNATO

I find it hard to defend veal, and so this is an adaptation of Vitello Tonnato, but it is hard to fault.

6 cooked chicken breasts with no skin
6 oz. canned tuna fish
6 anchovy fillets
1 teaspoon of capers
2 tablespoons of caperberries
juice of ½ lemon
ground black pepper
8-oz. jar of Hellmann's mayonnaise

Slice the chicken thinly as though you were slicing it off the bone. Lay out down the centre of the serving dish (preferably a plain white one). To make the sauce put the tuna fish, anchovy fillets, capers and lemon juice into a blender and mix. Add mayonnaise and blend again. Add more lemon juice if this is too thick. Pour the sauce over the chicken slices and sprinkle with caperberries. Serve with a green salad and new potatoes with parsley.

Serves 6

LOBSTER SALAD

Lobsters are so expensive that I hardly dare write this down, but this was one of the best lunch dishes I have ever had. Dubrovnik, before all the bombs and horrors, was quite lovely and I was taken by the Yugoslav Tourist Board for lunch in a little fish restaurant down the coast. It smelt of barbecued fish and rosemary and it was there that we had this amazing salad. I am making up the quantities, as I have no real idea of what the chef used. As in the case of Kenneth Lane's caviar recipe, buy as much lobster as you can afford!

4 boiled lobsters cut into pieces, leaving the claws whole
1 red onion sliced
2 lbs. of potatoes, boiled and sliced
½ cup virgin olive oil
juice of one lemon
salt and pepper to taste

and... the magic ingredient, a little fresh shredded sage

Put the hot potatoes into a dish with the onions, sage, olive oil, salt and pepper. Pour the lemon juice over the lobster and then mix with the other ingredients. The hot potatoes should half-warm the lobster. It is poetry.

Serves 6

DUNCAN MCLAREN'S
LEFTOVERS

My beloved friend Duncan McLaren, great traveller that he is, always wants leftovers on Sunday nights or when he feels in need of comfort food. He maintains that all food tastes better cold! When I told him I was preparing this book he insisted that his favourite recipe should be included.

I am not sure how many votes of confidence I am going to get on this one. There is no exact recipe - just use what you have.

cold potatoes
cold ham
cold broad beans
skinned tomatoes
butter
salt and pepper

Chop everything up and fry in butter for approx. 20 mins. and serve!

FILLET OF **BEEF** ROLLED IN **BLACK PEPPER**

As I am not a great meat eater, this is not one of my favourite recipes, but it seems to be popular and is quick and easy - and expensive!

whole fillet of beef
4 oz. black peppercorns
soya sauce
olive oil

Either grind or crush the peppercorns. Soak the fillet of beef in soya sauce and a little olive oil for at least 1 hr. It is even better if you can leave it in the fridge overnight with a little clove of garlic.

Take the fillet out of the soya sauce and dry. Coat with a little more olive oil and then roll in the crushed peppercorns until thickly coated. Bake in a very hot oven for 25 mins. Allow to stand for 5 mins. before putting on a serving plate and slicing.

This can be served with lots of different sauces, such as hollandaise, mushroom or bordelais.

Serves 8

Baked **APPLES**

A very English pudding which is nice in winter
and easy to make.

8 green cooking apples
1 pkt. sultanas
one 340-g. tin of golden syrup

Core the apples, leaving a hole of about 1½ in.
down the middle. Fill with sultanas. Put in a
greased baking dish and cover with golden syrup.
Bake in a medium oven for 1½ hours, basting
once or twice.

Serves 8

Rösti with Leeks, Sour Cream and Lumpfish Roe

One can now buy delicious rösti in a packet. This is one way to use it. It can serve as a main course for lunch or if you are feeling like something filling when not eating meat.

2 pkts. of rösti
1 tablespoon of vegetable oil
4 large leeks
¼ pt. of sour cream
2 oz. of either black or red lumpfish roe
salt
ground black pepper

Cut the rösti into square pieces, about 4 ins. square. Sauté in vegetable oil until brown and crispy. Keep warm. Boil the leeks, drain and place them on the rösti with a tablespoon of sour cream on the top. Finally, put a teaspoon of either black or red lumpfish roe on the sour cream to decorate and then sprinkle the whole with black pepper.

Serves 4

Sautéed **COD** with **TOMATOES** and **GRAPES**

I have always thought that grapes go very well with tomatoes, and this is an example.

6 cod steaks
½ pt. tomato sauce
1 bunch seedless white grapes cut in half
2 tablespoons olive oil
2 oz. butter
½ onion finely chopped
1 clove of garlic finely chopped
juice of ¼ lemon
salt and pepper

Fry the garlic and onion in the olive oil and butter. Add the cod steaks and cook until just brown on one side. In another pan heat tomato sauce and grapes. Put the cod steaks onto a serving dish and squeeze the lemon on them with some salt and pepper. Pour the tomatoes and grapes over them and serve with fluffy white rice and a green vegetable.

Serves 6

POTATOES COOKED WITH BAY LEAVES AND TOMATO

This is very good served with a roast. The bay leaves have a distinct, clean flavour. If possible, cook in a white ovenware dish and serve alongside a green vegetable.

10 large white potatoes
8 bay leaves
3 tins of chopped tomatoes
2 tablespoons of sundried tomato paste
salt and pepper
½ cup olive oil

Peel the potatoes and slice into 1-in. thick pieces. Boil in salted water until just soft. Drain and allow to sit in a colander until fluffy at the edges. Grease a large ovenproof dish with a little oil and put in a layer of potato. Dust with black pepper and cover with some chopped tomatoes.

Add a couple of bay leaves between each layer. Repeat the process and make sure the potatoes are covered with tomatoes on the top. Then pour over the remaining olive oil. Bake in a hot oven for 45 mins.

Serves 8

Roast **VEGETABLE PASTA**

One of the most organized people I know, Mrs Gordon Jones, gave me this recipe. She is a wonderful cook and seems to create endless delicacies, after having done a thousand other things all day.

4 red peppers
8 oz. courgettes
8 oz. aubergines (about 2 large ones)
2 sticks of celery
8 oz. tomatoes
4 garlic cloves
2 tablespoons of olive oil
salt and pepper
4 oz. penne
4 oz. feta cheese
2 teaspoons balsamic vinegar

Cut the peppers, courgettes, aubergines and celery into bite-size pieces. Halve the tomatoes. Place all the vegetables, except for the tomatoes, in a roasting pan with garlic and oil. Cook them at 230°C for 40 mins. until tender and well charred, adding the tomatoes for the last 20 mins.

About 15 mins. before the vegetables are ready, cook the pasta and drain. Crumble the feta cheese. Toss the pasta, cheese, vegetables with balsamic vinegar and plenty of salt and pepper.

Serves 6

Marinated **KIPPERS** WITH **RED KIDNEY BEANS**

A good and easy starter. I got this recipe from a girl friend years ago and I must say that it has got me out of several tight corners. Substitute tuna fish for the kippers if necessary but treat it the same way.

4 kipper fillets
olive oil
juice of a whole lemon
1 tin of red kidney beans
2 white onions
chopped parsley

Cut the kipper fillets into small strips. Put on the dish you are going to serve this in and cover with 4 tablespoons of olive oil. Then pour over it the lemon juice and some freshly ground black pepper. Slice the onions very thin and put on top. Cover with cling film and allow to sit for several hours. Mix in the kidney beans and serve with the chopped parsley on top.

Serves 4

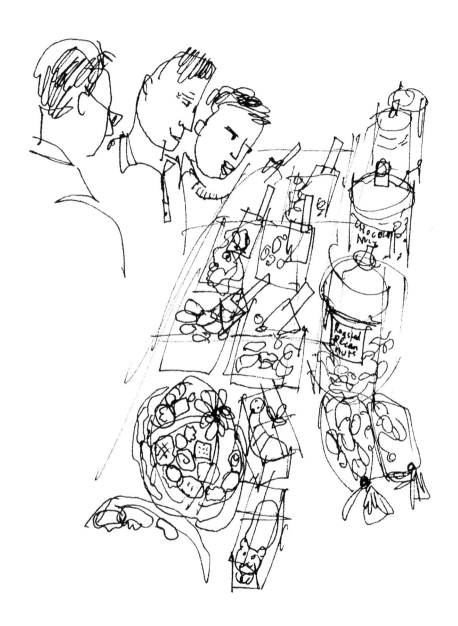

LEMON CURD OMELET

This is a delicious pudding if you are cooking in your kitchen with your guests or have a cook. It is difficult to time otherwise.

8 beaten eggs
half an 8-oz. jar of lemon curd
icing sugar

Lightly grease a non-stick frying pan and put onto medium/high heat. Pour in eggs and allow to cook. The bottom of the omelet should be golden brown and the middle nearly set. Smooth the lemon curd over half of the omelet, allow it to warm, then fold over onto your serving plate. Sift 2 tablespoons of icing sugar onto the omelet and serve immediately.

Serves 4

Spaghetti Gorgonzola
EN PAPILLOTE

A recipe from Mark Wogan, TV and newspaper chef:

'Jennifer's kitchen is always a hive of activity, in which (whenever I'm there) I find myself somehow involved. This is usually due to her phobia about touching raw meat. I'm invariably greeted with a charming smile and a piece of sirloin, followed by a request to "deal with it!". Rumour has it that she used to weep in the butcher's shop as a child. When she asked me to contribute to her cooking volume, I felt it was only right that the dish should be meat-free, just in case I wasn't around to help her try it out!

225 g. dried spaghetti
2 cloves of garlic, crushed
350 ml. double cream
150 g. gorgonzola cheese
black pepper
2 tablespoons chopped fresh parsley

Boil the pasta in salted water until just tender, drain and rinse under a cold running tap. Put the cream and garlic in a pan and bring to the boil. Remove from the heat, crumble in the cheese and stir it until melted. Season with the black pepper and add the parsley. Mix the pasta and cheese sauce together.

Cut four 30-cm. circles of tin foil and place equal amount of the pasta in the centre of each one. Seal up the parcels tightly, making sure you leave a small pocket of air in them. Also be careful not to puncture the foil. Place in a preheated oven at 190°C for 15 mins. Remove, split the bags open and serve.

Gorgonzola has a distinct flavour similar to that of Stilton. This is a very rich dish but also very satisfying.'

Serves 4

Marrons PURÉE
DESSERT

For those lucky people who can eat rich desserts this is a joy, but it should really be served only after a light meal. It is quick and easy to make and looks good served in a clear glass bowl. You can serve it either cold or at room temperature.

two 8-oz. tins of puréed chestnuts
1 pt. stiffly whipped cream
3 dessertspoons of castor sugar
2 large tablespoons of cocoa powder

Put the pureed chestnuts into a deep bowl. Mix slowly with an electric beater, while adding the sugar, until smooth. Fold in the cream so that the mixture is still brown and white, and spoon into a serving dish. Leave the top in peaks and sprinkle with cocoa powder.

Serves 8

Goat Cheese
WITH **CHILLIES** IN OLIVE OIL

The Hôtel des Arcades in Biot is where I found this wonderful dish. It is dead easy to make and is unusual looking. Serve at the end of lunch or dinner with a mixed green salad and French bread.

1½ pts. of virgin olive oil
two 6-in. long round goat cheeses with skin on
½ cup red dried chillies
10 bay leaves (preferably fresh)
1 large sprig of thyme or 6 little ones

Put the olive oil into a dessert-sized glass bowl. Cut cheese into ½ in. thick slices and add to the oil. Then add the chillies, bay leaves and thyme, making sure that everything is under the oil. Leave covered for at least 24 hrs. at room temperature.

Serves 8

Pan Fried **COD** with **EGG SAUCE**

This is a very old English dish which is not often seen nowadays. My son always eats it at Swinley Forest Golf Club. I think they poach the cod, but I prefer it pan fried.

1½ lbs. of skinless, boneless cod fillet
1 oz. butter
salt and pepper
4 hard-boiled eggs chopped finely
½ pt. white sauce

Cut the cod fillet into 4 pieces and pan fry until golden on one side.

Make the white sauce and add the chopped hard-boiled eggs and plenty of black pepper. Serve the cod (preferably not on a white dish) with the sauce on the side.

Serves 4

ROAST **PORK LOIN FILLET** WITH ORANGE SAUCE

This is a great favourite in our house, hot or cold. It makes a very good Sunday lunch and is delicious cold. I usually serve it with cauliflower cheese or leeks in cheese sauce and either roast or new potatoes.

2 smoked pork loin fillets from any of the supermarkets
2 tablespoons brown sugar
English mustard
1 small jar of red currant jelly
1 pt. fresh orange juice
squeeze of lemon
pepper

Cover the pork fillets with English mustard and sprinkle on sugar, making a crust. Bake in oven at 170°C for 1 hr. and 15 mins. until brown. Allow to sit for a few minutes before carving. Slice very thinly and serve with orange sauce. Alternatively, slice the 2 joints and lay out on a dish and pour the sauce over them.

The orange sauce is a good cheat. Add the currant jelly to the orange juice and put on a low heat until dissolved. Add a squeeze of lemon and a dash of pepper.

Serves 8

Baked BANANAS

There are endless ways of cooking bananas. This is my way.

12 ripe bananas
1 oz. butter
8-oz. tin of golden syrup
4 oz. soft brown sugar
juice of ½ lemon

Cut the bananas in circles and place in a baking dish with knobs of butter. Cover with golden syrup. Pour over the lemon juice. Sprinkle with brown sugar and put into a very hot oven for ½ hr. If the sugar has not caramelized, put under a hot grill until brown.

Serves 6

Semolina, HAM AND PARSLEY SOUFFLÉ

Every time I used to see the word soufflé in a cookery book I would think Help! it's too difficult for me. As I learned, soufflés are not difficult if you remember two things. One is to fill the dish to the top and the other is to beat the egg whites until they are really stiff. This recipe is useful for a ladies' lunch or for four people at dinner. I have never had the confidence to cook two of them in one oven.

4 cups of milk
1½ cups of semolina
1 oz. butter
4 eggs, separated
2 oz. grated parmesan
2 oz. finely chopped lean boiled ham
handful of finely chopped parsley
salt and pepper

Bring the milk to the boil. Pour the semolina over the surface and cook, stirring all the time, for about 20 mins. over a moderate heat. Season, and stir in the butter. Leave to cool.

Beat the egg whites stiff. When semolina mixture is cool, stir in the beaten egg yolks. Next mix in the ham, parmesan and parsley. Lastly, fold in the beaten egg whites. Put into a greased soufflé dish and bake in the oven for 30 mins. at 400°F or 200°C. Serve immediately.

Serves 6

GRILLED **PLAICE** WITH PESTO SAUCE AND **PINE NUTS**

A very simple fish dish with charm. Serve with a light green salad and boiled potatoes without their skins.

6 whole fillets of plaice
1 tub of fresh pesto sauce
salt and pepper
1 pkt. of pine nuts

Put pine nuts on a baking tray and grill until slightly brown, turning several times. Place fillets on a lightly greased sheet of tinfoil on a baking tray. Cover each fillet with pesto sauce and a little salt and pepper. Cook for 4 mins. and cover with the pine nuts.

Serves 6

STUFFED **EGGS** SERVED WITH **SMOKED HAM** AND ROCKET

This is always a winner! It's a great favourite as a starter for Sunday lunch and you can always vary the bits and pieces you serve it with, such as baby tomatoes, black olives, celery sticks and caperberries. Even I have never managed to make a mess of hard-boiled eggs.

10 hard-boiled eggs
1 bunch spring onions
6-oz. jar of mayonnaise
salt and pepper
2 pkts. of very finely sliced chargrilled smoked ham
1 bunch of rocket
1 bunch of chives

Cut the hard-boiled eggs in half and place the yolks in a mixing bowl. Mash them finely, adding salt, pepper, chopped spring onions and mayonnaise. Mix well and heap into the egg whites. Cover with chopped chives. Place on a serving dish and surround with sliced ham and rocket.

Serves 8

ARTICHOKE HEARTS AND **PRAWNS** IN A CHEESE SAUCE

Quick and easy. Very good on a Sunday night or if you have to rustle up something in a hurry. You can substitute various other vegetables, such as cabbage, broccoli or cauliflower.

2 tins artichoke hearts
1 lb. peeled prawns
1½ pts. of thick cheese sauce
grated parmesan
12 slices of very thin streaky bacon

Drain the artichoke hearts. Put into an ovenproof dish and mix in the prawns. Cover with the cheese sauce. Lay the rashers of bacon crisscross over the top and sprinkle with parmesan. Cook in a medium hot oven for 40 mins. and then finish under a hot grill. Bacon should be crisp and the top of the sauce golden brown.

Serves 8

POTATO SALAD

I love potato salad. In fact, I love potatoes. I think I should really have written a potato cook book. However, pages are money, so I am going to give you 2 recipes, one of mine and one of Nicky Haslam's. His is better served with just a green salad and mine can be served with any summer salad.

NICKY HASLAM'S
POTATO SALAD

2 lbs. of new potatoes
1 chorizo sausage
olive oil
salt and pepper
a bunch of spring onions

Boil the potatoes until soft, then allow to cool. Cut chorizo into ½ in. bites. Cut potatoes into halves and put into a large salad bowl. Season and dribble olive oil over them and mix in the chorizo and chopped chives. Serve with a green salad.

Serves 6

MY
POTATO SALAD

2 lbs. of new potatoes
a bunch of chives
a small tub of black olives with herbs
a large bunch of parsley
½ cup of vinaigrette made with grainy mustard

Boil the potatoes until soft, then allow to cool. Chop the parsley and chives very roughly. Cover the cooled potatoes with vinaigrette and mix in half the herbs. Sprinkle on the rest of the herbs and toss lightly. Add the olives just before serving, otherwise they mark the potatoes.

Serves 8 with another salad

Potted **SHRIMPS**

Potted shrimps are one of my favourite things. In the past few years, however, they seem to have changed for the worse. By accident I have discovered how to make them. I was buying some fish from the fish stall under the restaurant Bibendum and happened to ask the nice young man, Simon, who was serving me whether he had any potted shrimps. He said sadly that he had run out of them, but suggested that I make my own! How, I asked. All very simple if you know how: this is what he told me to do, and it has been a huge success.

3 pkts. (or ½ lb.) of crevettes grises
2 tablespoons of lemon juice
8 oz. butter
ground black pepper
a pinch of ground mace

Put the shrimps into a flat baking tin approx. 10 x 6 in., lined with foil. Melt the butter in a pan and add a squeeze of lemon, mace and black pepper. Pour the butter over the shrimps. The butter should not cover them but just hold them together. Put into the fridge for several hours. Take out the pan and slice the buttered shrimps into whatever size you like, and serve with hot toast or on hot blinis.

Serves 6

POULET
AU CHEMISE VERTE

Mark Walford, of Richards and Walford, great wine importers and suppliers to London top restaurants, is a very good and inventive cook. He kindly gave me this and the following recipe, both of which I have had great fun with. He travels France for half of every year looking for new and old wines and eats in many different places. He also makes the most wonderful home-made bread, something I have never been able to cope with.

6-7 lbs. free range chicken

Stuffing:

large handful of chopped parsley
small handful of chopped chives
small handful of chopped tarragon
large handful of chopped mushrooms
2 shallots, chopped
2 large cloves of garlic, chopped
½ pt. low-fat live yoghurt
salt and ground pepper
1 tablespoon olive or other good oil

Put all the stuffing ingredients in a bowl and mix by hand. Carefully lift the skin of the chicken by putting your fingers between its flesh and the skin of the breast and legs. This is easily done, but be careful not to tear the skin.

Spread the stuffing evenly between the breast and the skin and push it up into the legs. Rub gently with oil and put the bird in very hot oven for 20 mins., then simmer in medium oven for 2 hrs. Chicken makes its own juice, which should be spooned over the breast every ½ hr. There will be plenty of juice to deglaze the pan with before serving. Drop some chopped parsley in the juice.

If cooked in fan oven, start at high temperature, then reduce to 140ºC. Put a dish of water in the bottom of the oven to stop dehydration.

Apologies and acknowledgments to Michel Guérard who used to do this chicken at Eugénie-les-Bains as part of his Minceur course.

Serves 6

SPATCHCOCK PARTRIDGES

This is a very easy way to cook partridges, or indeed pigeons, and leave them with all their flavour. I like eating them with my fingers.

6 partridges
tablespoon of olive oil
salt and pepper

For the gravy:

backbones of partridges
2 tomatoes, peeled and chopped
1 shallot, chopped
large clove of garlic
2 glasses white wine
½ pint water

After cutting out their backbones, flatten the birds. Put them in a roasting dish with oil, salt and coarse ground pepper. Roast in a very hot oven for 10 mins., then rest for 10 mins. in a medium oven.

Put all the ingredients for the gravy into a pan, bring to the boil and reduce for ½ hr.

Serve with boiled, baked or mashed potatoes and a green vegetable. If you like game, this is a very good recipe indeed.

Serves 6

A DIFFERENT KIND OF **CHICKEN SALAD** WITH ROCKET

This can be used as a main course or a starter for lunch. It doesn't sound like much when written down but, believe me, it is special. The trick is to use really good, thick, hand-beaten mayonnaise. I serve it with boiled new potatoes.

6 cooked chicken breasts
½ pt. of thick homemade mayonnaise
2 bunches of rocket
roasted split almonds

Shred the chicken like crispy duck in a Chinese restaurant. Mix together with the mayonnaise and rocket. Brown the almonds in the oven and allow to cool. Sprinkle them over the salad.

Serves 6

BAKED **POTATOES** WITH **OLIVE OIL** AND **BASIL**

Baked potatoes are comfort food to me. These are delicious served with cold meats and salad, or just on their own.

4 large baking potatoes
1 bunch of basil
olive oil
salt and pepper

Wash and dry the potatoes. Cut a slice off the top of them, leaving a flat plateau. Grease them lightly and cook until the skin is crisp. Remove from the oven, cut open and scoop out the white flesh into a bowl. Add finely chopped basil, ½ cup virgin olive oil, salt and pepper, and mix well. Put the mixture back into the skins and bake for a further 15 mins.

Serves 4

COLD **CHEESE** SOUFFLÉ

This is a rather old-fashioned, proper dinner party recipe. It looks very good in little ramekin dishes.

2 oz. finely grated parmesan
2 eggs
½ pint cream, medium whipped
salt and pepper
3 oz. breadcrumbs toasted with dried basil

Separate the eggs. Whip the whites until very stiff. Beat the yolks until creamy and add the parmesan and seasoning. Fold in the cream and then the egg whites. Place in a soufflé dish and chill overnight. Cook the breadcrumbs with a little oil and dried basil until golden brown. Allow to cool. Sprinkle them over the soufflé just before serving.

Serves 4

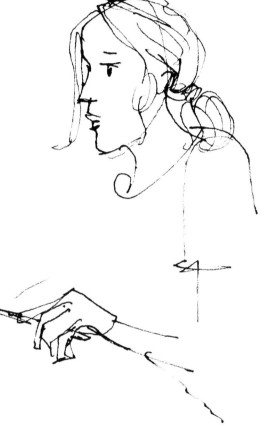

Dried FRUIT PLATTER WITH CAMEMBERT AND BRIOCHES

During the winter months, when there seems to be a lot of dried fruit in the shops, this makes an interesting end to a meal. Make sure that you serve it on a pretty dish and heap up the fruit.

8 small brioches
1 large very ripe camembert
dried figs, apricots, dates, sultanas and pineapple slices

Place the camembert in the centre of the serving dish and surround it with all the dried fruit. Keep the fruit separate. Warm the brioches and serve in a basket.

Serves 6

FLAGEOLET BEAN AND WATERCRESS SOUP

Comfort soup!

2 tins green flageolet beans
2 large onions, chopped
2 bunches of watercress, chopped
1 clove of garlic
1 tablespoon of olive oil
1½ pts. of vegetable stock
salt and pepper

Sauté the chopped garlic and onion in olive oil until soft. Add all the other ingredients and simmer until the soup has thickened. Serve with croutons or herb bread.

Serves 6

CAESAR SALAD

When I asked my son Joel Cadbury, the well-known young restaurateur, for a recipe for this book, I was rather hoping he would come up with something I had taught him. No such luck! He went to learn to cook with arguably London's best chef, Gordon Ramsay. Gordon despaired of Joel's culinary talents and sent him packing. This delicious recipe is what he learned.

¼ **pt. mayonnaise**
juice of ½ **lemon**
2 cloves garlic, crushed
2 cloves garlic, halved
1 oz. grated parmesan
12 anchovy fillets
salt and pepper
½ **head iceberg lettuce**
½ **head cos lettuce**
4 slices of thick white bread
4 fl. oz. olive oil

Put the mayonnaise, lemon juice, crushed garlic and 6 anchovy fillets in the liquidizer and blend until smooth. Chop the remaining 6 anchovy fillets and fold into the Caesar sauce. Thin down if necessary with a little water.

Heat the olive oil slowly with the halved garlic cloves. Remove the crusts from the bread, cut into cubes and fry in the oil until golden, then drain on kitchen paper. Season and sprinkle with a little parmesan while still warm.

Prepare the lettuces and toss with the dressing and the rest of the parmesan, place in a bowl and sprinkle with the croutons.

Serves 4 to 6

Baked TOMATOES WITH MOZZARELLA AND ANCHOVIES

This can be used hot or cold and is a useful starter. Some people do not eat anchovies, so it can be done instead with tiny shreds of bacon.

4 large beefsteak tomatoes
2 buffalo mozzarellas
1 tin anchovy fillets
salt and pepper
dried basil flakes

Cut the tomatoes in half. Place in a greased baking dish. Sprinkle with salt, pepper and dried basil flakes and a little olive oil. Cut the mozzarella in slices and put on top of the tomatoes. Place the anchovies crisscrossed on the cheese. Bake for $\frac{1}{2}$ hr. in a medium oven until the cheese starts to go golden.

Serves 8

PORK NOISETTES
WITH PRUNES

This dish is traditionally served with boiled
potatoes only. I suggest, if possible, they should
surround the meat in the French style.

two 8-oz. tins of prunes
6 pieces of pork fillet approx. 3 ins. long
½ bottle of dry white wine
seasoned flour
2 oz. butter
1 heaped tablespoon of redcurrant jelly
¾ pt. of double cream
salt and black pepper
juice of ½ lemon

Puree one tin of prunes in the blender and drain
the other one, keeping the prunes to arrange
with the meat. Mix the puree with the wine. Coat
the fillet of pork in seasoned flour and fry in
butter gently over a low heat until cooked
(approx. 15 mins.). Keep warm.

Put the puree and redcurrant jelly in a pan and
stir over a high heat until the jelly is melted.
Gradually blend in the cream and stir until the
sauce is smooth and thick. Season with lemon
juice, salt and pepper. Add the remaining prunes
to warm and then pour over the pork.

Serves 6

BRANDY SNAP BASKETS WITH STRAWBERRIES

This is not original or clever but it is a good mix of flavours and looks pretty. Do not serve it with cream; I think it is better just served with a few sprigs of mint.

8 brandy snap baskets (which can be bought in packets)
1 lb. strawberries
¼ pt. plain chocolate sauce
¼ pt. raspberry coulis

Slice the strawberries and heap them into the brandy snap baskets. Pour chocolate sauce on the top. Put them on individual plates and surround them with raspberry coulis. If you prefer to serve them on a large plate, serve the coulis on the side.

Serves 8

CRABSTICK AND **CELERIAC** SALAD

This is a light and easy starter, one of those things I throw together if I'm very short of time. When you serve it, you can only hope that no one at the table is allergic to shellfish!

500 g. shredded celeriac
10 crabsticks
½ cup mayonnaise
black pepper
½ teaspoon turmeric

Mix the mayonnaise with the turmeric and black pepper. Toss the celeriac in the mixture. Cut the crabsticks into thin strips about 1½-in. wide and add. Do not let the crabsticks get smothered by the mayonnaise as they look prettier when pink.

Serves 6

CHICKEN AND **GRAPE** SALAD WITH PARSLEY VINAIGRETTE

A quick and simple summer dish. I usually serve it with a radicchio salad on the side and new potatoes.

6 cold chicken breasts
1 large bunch of seedless white grapes
1 large bunch of parsley
½ cup vinaigrette made with *moutarde de Maille à l'ancienne*

Chop the chicken into cubes. Cut the grapes in half. Chop the parsley, not too finely. Pour the vinaigrette onto the chicken and mix in the parsley. Add the grapes last and toss only once or twice as they look better if they are not covered in parsley.

Serves 6

CAULIFLOWER WITH CURRIED MAYONNAISE, ROCKET AND PINE NUTS

Not good for the figure but a good starter for lunch or dinner. Serve on a flat plate with hot bread.

1 large cauliflower
2 tablespoons creme fraiche
6 tablespoons mayonnaise
1 teaspoon curry paste
1 pkt. rocket
1 pkt. pine nuts

Cut fleurets off the cauliflower and slice into thin strips. Blanch in salted boiling water for 4 mins. and drain. Rinse under cold water. Mix mayonnaise with 2 tablespoons creme fraiche and curry paste. Add more curry paste for personal taste. Put pine nuts on tinfoil in a dish in a hot oven. Keep turning until brown. When cauliflower is cold, mix with mayonnaise mixture. Place on serving dish and put the rocket around the edge. Cover with pine nuts.

Serves 4

COLD WHITING WITH CHOPPED TOMATOES AND BASIL OIL

A wonderful summer dish. I had this at lunch with Jane Churchill and thought it was one of the best things I have ever eaten. I always remember whiting from my childhood because it was served, deep-fried, with its tail in its mouth! Whiting is not an easy fish to buy but it is well worth the effort to seek it out. In need, the recipe can be made with sole.

8 whiting fillets (skinned and boned)
white wine
6 beefsteak tomatoes, skinned and chopped
4 tablespoons of light vinaigrette
chopped chives
salt and black pepper
basil oil

Fold the whitings in half, wrap them in tinfoil and poach in a little white wine. Allow to cool. Chop the tomatoes and make a small amount of vinaigrette and mix together with salt and a generous helping of black pepper.

Place the whitings on the serving dish and sprinkle with the tomato mixture and then the chives. Pour a little basil oil around the bottom of each fillet. Serve with warm brown bread.

Serves 8

CABBAGE AND SHITAKE MUSHROOMS

Mixed vegetable dishes can often lift rather plain food, and they also make for interesting flavours.

1 white cabbage, shredded finely
2 large cloves of garlic, crushed
6 oz. shitake mushrooms
1 bunch parsley, finely chopped
2 tablespoons safflower oil
salt and pepper

Fry garlic in oil and then gently fry the mushrooms until just tender. Remove from pan. Rinse the cabbage, season and put into the frying pan with the remaining hot oil. Add a little more oil if necessary. Toss the cabbage over high heat being careful not to brown it. When it is just soft, add lots of black pepper and the mushrooms. Mix together over the heat and sprinkle with parsley.

Serves 6

CURRIED **POTATOES**

I think this is a delicious way to cook potatoes. It
is very good with lamb or anything spicy.

10 large roasting potatoes
1 tablespoon hot curry paste
1 large clove of garlic
2 large onions
½ cup sultanas
½ pt. vegetable stock
olive oil
salt and pepper

Peel the potatoes and slice into thick slices. Boil
until just tender and then drain. Put the sliced
onion, garlic and curry paste into a frying pan
and fry in a little oil until just soft.

Make stock from cube and ½ pt. hot water. Mix
with the onions. Put potatoes into a greased
ovenproof dish, mixing in the sultanas, and pour
the liquid mixture over it, making sure that the
onions are not all on the top. Dribble on a little
olive oil and bake in a hot oven until brown,
approx. 45 mins.

Serves 8

SALMON CRU SERVED WITH PINK GINGER
AND BLACK BREAD

This is a good starter for a dinner party. The pink ginger is pickled and therefore not too hot to ruin the taste buds for the main course.

10 oz. raw salmon fillet
juice of ½ lemon
black pepper
Japanese pink pickled ginger
black bread (I suggest the German
pumpernickel available in packets)
1 pkt. rocket
1 bunch of chives, chopped

Put the salmon in a blender and blend until it is still in small pieces and sticking together but not paste. Mix in lemon juice and black pepper and some of the chopped chives. Take out a tablespoon at a time and pat into balls.

Cut black bread into 2-in. squares. Put the salmon balls onto the bread squares and flatten them a little. Put 2 or 3 slices of pink ginger on each one. Decorate with remaining chives. When you have laid the salmon out on the serving plate, place the rocket around the dish.

Serves 8

Mini-Cauliflower AND CABBAGE
VINAIGRETTE

This is a Jennifer special! It is not at all difficult to do and looks attractive. It is quite easy to buy mini-cauliflowers but not always so easy to get the miniature cabbages. I sometimes use similar-sized broccoli fleurets. It is not a disaster if you use just one vegetable.

If you want to make this dish extra special, put some parma ham or salami around the edge of the dish. Otherwise decorate just with the rocket.

Serves 8

4 mini-cauliflowers
4 mini-cabbages
¼ lb. thinly sliced parmesan
balsamic vinegar
virgin olive oil, or better still, basil oil
salt and pepper
1 bunch of rocket

Cut the bottoms off the cauliflowers and the cabbages. Cut a cross on the top of the cabbages about ½ in. deep. Put both vegetables into boiling salted water and cook until just soft. Drain and run under very cold water. Allow to drain completely in a cool place and then, if possible, put in the fridge for an hour.

Set the vegetables out on a flat serving dish and dribble olive oil over each one. Then dribble balsamic vinegar through the middle of the cabbages. DO NOT put vinegar on the cauliflowers. Then put balsamic vinegar round the bottom of each vegetable so that it makes a pretty pattern with the oil. Sprinkle with black pepper and put the parmesan over them.

GRILLED **AVOCADOES** WITH **PRAWNS** GRATINÉE

This is best made when you can find really good avocadoes. It is a good starter for a dinner party, as you can prepare the avocadoes in advance and just put them under the grill at the last minute.

4 large ripe avocadoes
6 ozs. prawns
½ pt. very thick cheese sauce
Dijon mustard
grated parmesan

Make cheese sauce with a generous addition of Dijon mustard. Put aside to go cold. Cut avocadoes in half and fill with prawns. Cover with a generous helping of cheese sauce. Dust with parmesan. Put under a hot grill until brown. Serve immediately.

Serves 8

MACARONI CHEESE WITH **TUNA, SUNDRIED TOMATOES** AND WHITE WINE

Comfort food. Not difficult and something you can pull out of the store cupboard if you have unexpected guests!

500 g. macaroni
two 200-g. tins of tuna fish
1 small jar of sundried tomatoes
½ lb. grated mature cheddar
English mustard
1½ pts. of milk
2 tablespoons of flour
salt and pepper
small glass of white wine
grated parmesan

Put macaroni into fast boiling salted water and cook until tender. Drain and put into large shallow baking dish. Drain and flake the tuna fish and mix with the pasta. Drain sundried tomatoes and chop into small pieces. Add to pasta. Make a thick cheese sauce with 2 large teaspoons of English mustard and add small glass of white wine. Do not put sauce over pasta until it is cold.

Cover pasta with sauce and sprinkle with parmesan. Bake in hot oven at 400°F until brown, approx. 30 mins. Serve with a green side salad or green beans at room temperature with a vinaigrette.

Serves 8

STUFFED **PORK** FILLET WITH A CREAMY **MUSTARD** SAUCE

This recipe was sent to me by Mrs Terry Wogan, who is a superb cook. She is one of those people who can cook for an army and appear looking beautiful and totally relaxed. The Wogan household is filled with a family of 'stars' and yet it is one of the most relaxed homes I have ever visited.

2 pork fillets
1 pkt. of rindless streaky bacon
2 shallots
1 clove of garlic
8 oz. chestnut mushrooms
3 oz. breadcrumbs
handful of sundried tomatoes
3 sprigs of basil
salt and pepper
2 tablespoons of olive oil

Sauce:

½ pt. chicken stock
½ pt. dry white wine
8-oz. carton of creme fraiche
1 tablespoon Dijon mustard
handful of chopped parsley

Chop the shallots and garlic and fry in olive oil. Chop mushrooms small but not too finely and add to pan. Cook quickly, add breadcrumbs. When slightly cool, add 1 egg to combine. Allow to go cold before putting on to meat. Add seasoning.

Put pork fillets on a flat surface and cut halfway along the centre. Press to flatten a little. Add stuffing to one fillet, lay a line of sundried tomatoes on top and then the basil leaves. Place the other fillet on top. Stretch the bacon slices with a small flat knife. Wrap the pork fillets with the bacon until completely covered. Place in a roasting dish, season the top and drizzle with olive oil. Preheat oven to 200ºC and cook at 190º for 1¼ hours. Take out of roasting dish and leave to rest for at least 10 mins. Drain off fat from roasting tin and reserve the remainder.

For the sauce, reduce the chicken stock and wine by half. Pour into roasting tin and scrape any nice brown pieces into the liquid, return to saucepan, add the carton of creme fraiche and boil until slightly thickened. Whisk in the mustard and add the parsley. Slice the pork about ½ in. thick, two slices per person. Put some of the sauce on the plate and place the pork slices on top. Serve the rest of the sauce on the side.

Serves 6

Chicken, Black Olive AND Cider Stew

I love black olives and use them all the time. This dish should be served with plain mashed potatoes and winter vegetables.

12 skinned and boned chicken thighs
2 apples, peeled and cored
1 pt. chicken stock
6 oz. stoned black olives with herbs
2 cloves of garlic chopped
1 cup cider
salt and pepper flour

Put some seasoned flour on a large plate and roll the chicken thighs in it.

Put oil and garlic into a pan and cook until garlic is turning golden. Add chicken thighs and fry gently until the outsides are cooked. This is to help them hold their shape.

Put the chicken into a casserole and cover with olives. Slice the apples very thin and add. Pour on stock and cider and cover with lid. Cook in a medium oven for 1 hr. and then turn down to low and cook for another hour, having stirred once. Leave to stand overnight.

Check in the morning and add more seasoning if necessary. Stir well and reheat.

Serves 6

CHOCOLATE BREAD PUDDING

Mrs·Henry Ford II gave me this recipe, saying it was too good to be missed. She is quite right and, what's more, it is easy to make.

10 slices brioche bread (or good day-old white bread), cut into triangles
6 oz. cooking chocolate
15 oz. whipping cream
4 tablespoons dark rum
4 oz. sugar
3 oz. butter
3 large eggs

Put chocolate, cream, sugar, rum and butter into a double boiler over boiling water and stir until sugar is completely dissolved. Take off heat and stir well.

Whisk eggs and add to chocolate mixture. Layer the bread in a baking (and serving) dish and cover with chocolate. Leave at room temperature for 2 hrs. and then put into fridge for 24 hrs.

Cook at 350°F for 30 to 35 mins. and serve.

Serves 8

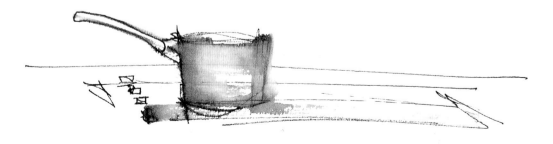

GOUGÈRES WITH CREAMED HADDOCK

To my mind, this is one of the best dishes I know. It sounds more difficult than it is, so try it when you have plenty of time. The second time will be easier.

4 oz. butter

4 eggs

6 oz. flour

3 oz. parmesan cheese

salt and pepper

8 oz. fillet of smoked haddock

½ pt. of thick white sauce

½ bunch of parsley, finely chopped

Place the butter with 10 fl. oz. of water in a heavy-bottomed pan and heat slowly. Bring to the boil and remove from the heat. Sift in the flour and return to low heat. Add parmesan and mix hard, until the mixture comes away from the side of the pan. Remove from the heat and add the beaten eggs, a little at a time. Mix until smooth, and add a little salt and pepper.

Using 2 teaspoons, put blobs of the mixture onto a greased sheet of tinfoil on a baking tray, making about 20 in all. Bake in a preheated oven for approx. 30 mins. at 400°F or 200°C. Do not open the oven door until 30 mins. is up. When they are a light golden brown, place them on a wire rack and allow to cool, having pricked each one with a sharp knife.

Make the white sauce and allow it to cool. Poach the haddock in a little milk, cool, drain off the milk and then flake. Chop the parsley and mix half of it into the white sauce. Add the haddock, and when completely cold fill the gougères with the mixture. Put back into the oven to reheat in a medium oven for 25 mins. Put on serving dish and sprinkle the remaining parsley over them.

Serves 8

EGG CROQUETTES
SERVED WITH TOMATO SAUCE

A favourite starter with my second husband, Peter Cadbury, who always said, when he had them, that he did not need anything else. Which was a reflection of how many he ate!... They can be made the day before, and are in fact better when made in advance.

10 hard-boiled eggs
1 pt. thick white sauce
fine white breadcrumbs
salt and pepper
vegetable oil
parsley
½ pt. tomato sauce
1 beaten egg

Chop the hard-boiled eggs. Mix with the white sauce which has salt and pepper added. Spread the mixture approx. 1 in. thick onto a greased baking tin and put into the fridge. Leave until very cold, preferably overnight.

Take out the mixture and cut into 3 x 1½-in. pieces. Pat into croquette shape, dip in the beaten egg and then roll in breadcrumbs. Heat some vegetable oil in a frying pan and shallow-fry the croquettes. When cooked, put them into the oven to keep warm. Served with fried parsley and tomato sauce.

Serves 6

BEEFSTEAK TOMATOES
WITH TOMATO ASPIC AND **PRAWNS**

A good starter or luncheon. In fact you can serve
it as a main course with new potatoes and
a green salad. Serve on a flat plate with
rocket on it.

8 large ripe beefsteak tomatoes
1 small bottle of clamato juice
juice of 1 lemon
1 oz. of gelatine
8 oz. peeled small prawns
bunch of parsley chopped
bunch of rocket

Blanch the tomatoes and peel them. Cut a circle
off the top of each one and hollow them out.
Dissolve the gelatine in $\frac{1}{2}$ cup of hot water and
allow to cool. Mix the gelatine and clamato juice,
and mix in the lemon juice and black pepper. Dry
the prawns, then put a tablespoon of them into
each tomato and cover with the clamato mixture.
Leave in the fridge for 4 hrs. and sprinkle with
parsley before serving. Put on a plain green or
clear dish and serve surrounded by rocket tossed
in a light vinaigrette.

Serves 8

INDEX

INDEX BY COURSES

Soups

Starters

Salads

Chicken salad with rocket 104
Crabmeat and celery salad 53
Crabstick and celeriac salad 113
Curried mushroom salad 28
Lobster salad 79
Pea salad 42
Potato salad (mine) 100
Potato salad (Nicky Haslam's) 100
Salad pavlovsk 72

Vegetable dishes

Baked potatoes with olive oil and basil 104
Baked tomatoes with mozzarella and anchovies 108
Beetroot mashed potatoes 66
Cabbage and shitake mushrooms 115
Cauliflower with curried mayonnaise 114
Curried potatoes 116
Goat cheese with chillies in olive oil 90
Goat cheese sandwich 41
Leeks with feta cheese and chilli vinaigrette 60
Mini-cauliflower and cabbage vinaigrette 118
Potatoes cooked with bay leaves
    and tomato 85
Roast vegetable pasta 86
Rolled stuffed omelet 44
Shallots cooked with bay leaves 16
Shirley Conran's warm bean salad 24
Vegetable curry 23

Pasta

Beetroot pasta 31
Macaroni cheese with tuna 119
Penne with yellow pepper coulis 37
Spaghetti gorgonzola en papillote 89
Spaghetti with anchovies and parsley 14
White spaghetti 39

Fish and seafood

Cod with chilli and shredded courgettes 73
Cold whiting with chopped tomatoes 114
Fillets of sole with saffron mayonnaise
    and fresh herbs 30
Fish stew 70
Gougères with creamed haddock 123
Grilled plaice with pesto sauce and pine nuts 97
Haddock Monte Carlo 62

Haddock, turmeric and spinach soup 59
Leek and salmon fish cakes 34
Lobster salad 79
Marinated kippers with red kidney beans 86
Pan fried cod with egg sauce 92
Potted shrimps 101
Salmon with pink ginger on a bed of spinach 42
Sautéed cod with tomatoes and grapes 84
Scallops with green Thai curry 51

Meat, poultry and game dishes

Chicken, black olive and cider stew 121
Chicken salad with rocket 104
Chicken tonnato 78
Duck with water chestnuts and green
    peppercorns 63
Fillet of beef rolled in black pepper 81
Galantine of chicken and ham 21
Michael Watson's duck 54
Pork noisettes with prunes 109
Poulet au chemise verte 102
Quail with marmalade and mustard 56
Roast pork loin fillet with orange sauce 95
Sausage meat loaf 68
Spatchcock partridges 103
Stuffed pork fillet with a creamy mustard sauce 120

Desserts

Baked apples 82
Baked bananas 96
Blenheim bombe 29
Brandy snap baskets with
    strawberries 110
Bread and butter pudding 20
Chocolate bread pudding 122
Chocolate nut crisps 27
Dried fruit platter with camembert
    and brioches 106
Drunken pineapple 69
Ginger biscuit pudding 77
Grape dessert 66
Lemon curd omelet 88
Lokshen kugel 32
Marrons purée dessert 90
Prune soufflé 50
Strawberries with mint 26
Wine jelly 38